CLEVELAND: VILLAGE TO METROPOLIS

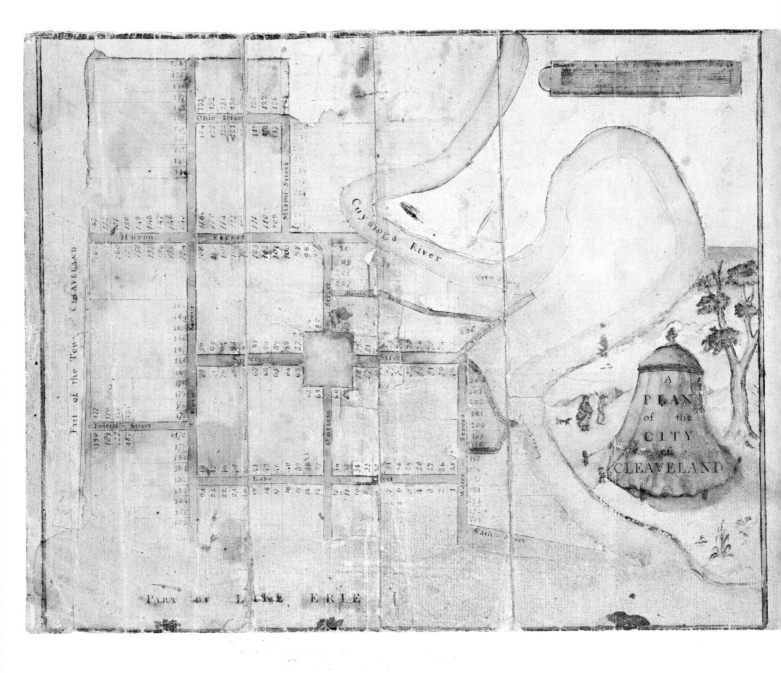

CLEVELAND:
VILLAGE TO METROPOLIS

A Case Study of Problems of Urban Development
in Nineteenth-century America

EDMUND H. CHAPMAN

A Joint Publication

THE WESTERN RESERVE HISTORICAL SOCIETY

THE PRESS OF WESTERN RESERVE UNIVERSITY

Dedicated to

WALTER W. S. COOKE

The Western Reserve Historical Society Publication Number 118

FRONTISPIECE: Second Plan of Cleaveland by Seth Pease, 1796. This fine water-color sketch, now in the Western Reserve Historical Society, was inverted by Pease so that Lake Erie appears at the bottom of the sheet.

ACKNOWLEDGEMENTS

With few exceptions the buildings of the first three quarters of the nineteenth century in Cleveland, with which this book is chiefly concerned, have disappeared, and in some cases new streets have effaced the original arrangements of the city plan. As a consequence a heavy burden has been placed upon the descriptions and occasional prints of the town in its early decades, and upon newspapers, directories and other records, and upon photographs for the period after 1850. The written and pictorial resources of the Cleveland Public Library and the Western Reserve Historical Society have been the principal sources for this history.

I am indebted to both of these institutions for their generous assistance in locating this material and for their permission to reproduce the illustrations here used. My especial thanks are due Mrs. Alene Lowe White, librarian of the Western Reserve Historical Society for her patience and skill in assisting my research.

The guidance and advice of Dr. Dimitris Tselos of the University of Minnesota and the constructive criticism of the late Professor Talbot Hamlin of Columbia University are gratefully acknowledged.

EDMUND H. CHAPMAN

September 4, 1964

CONTENTS

CATALOGUE OF ILLUSTRATIONS

Figure 1. The first plan of Cleveland, unsigned but endorsed in the handwriting of Amos Spafford: "Original Plan of the Town and Village of Cleaveland, Ohio, October 1st, 1796." The original of this map is in the Western Reserve Historical Society, volume one of maps, page one. Baker, *op. cit.*, 223, states that this map was discovered among the papers of J. Milton Holley and sent to Charles Whittlesey by his son, Alexander H. Holley.

Figure 2. The mouth of the Cuyahoga River in 1800. From the original, anonymous drawing now in the Western Reserve Historical Society.

Figure 3. Plan of Cleveland in 1814. This copy of Spafford's map of 1801 was made by Alfred Kelley in 1814 to show the location of houses in the town at that time. The indications of shore-line changes were added by Whittlesey. From Whittlesey, *Early History*, etc., 434.

Figure 4. The first Court House in Cleveland. This water-color painting now in the Western Reserve Historical Society is based on a painting by Otto Ruetinek which was in turn executed from a pencil sketch of the building by a man by the name of Waterman which was, according to Orth, in the possession of F. S. Barnum in 1910.

Figure 5. Street development of Cleveland, 1815-1830. This plan is based on that of Spafford in 1801 with the new streets added. Tracing by William Hazen and Robert Warner.

Figure 6. Plan of Cleveland, showing annexations. From Orth, *op. cit.*, I, opp. p. 46.

Figure 7. Alfred Kelley residence, 1814-17. From a print in the Western Reserve Historical Society.

Figure 8. The Academy, 1821-2. From a drawing in the Western Reserve Historical Society.

Figure 9. The first Franklin House, Cleveland, 1826, Philo Scovill, architect. From a print in the Western Reserve Historical Society.

Figure 10. The Public Square, Cleveland, 1839. From a painting in the Western Reserve Historical Society attributed to Sebastian Heine.

Figure 11. The Second Court House, Cleveland, 1828. This is the main facade as it appeared in the late 1850's just prior to removal. From a stereopticon pair in the Western Reserve Historical Society.

Figure 12. Trinity Church, Cleveland, 1828-29. From an enlarged and retouched detail of a lithograph of the city looking east from St. Clair and Bank Streets. Reproduced by the courtesy of the Cleveland Public Library.

Figure 13. Plan of Trinity Church, 1828-29. The location of the staircase and the structural details of the entrance and the interior supports of the tower are hypothetical. Drawn by William Hazen and Robert Warner.

Figure 14. Plan of Cleveland, 1835, from an actual survey by Ahaz Merchant. From a print of the original now in the Western Reserve Historical Society.

Figure 15. Plan of the City of Cleveland, 1853. From the frontispiece of Knight and Parsons, *Business Directory of the City of Cleveland*. Cleveland, 1853.

Figure 16. Cleveland from Brooklyn Hill, looking east, 1833.

From an original lithograph by Thomas Whelpley now in the Western Reserve Historical Society.

Figure 69. The Kennard House, Cleveland, erected in 1855 as the Angier House, remodelled as the Kennard House, in 1866. From a photograph, dated 1876, in the Western Reserve Historical Society.

Figure 70. New Court House, Cleveland, erected in 1858, J. J. Husband, architect. Photograph of 1935, taken during demolition, now in the Cleveland Public Library.

Figure 71. Union Passenger Depot, Cleveland, erected in 1864-66. From a print in Payne, *op. cit.,* 29.

Figure 72. New Court House. From a photograph in the Cleveland Public Library.

Figure 73. Federal Building, Cleveland, erected in 1859, Ammi B. Young, architect; W. J. Warner, builder. From a print in Payne, *op. cit.,* 125.

Figure 74. Federal Building, Cleveland, in 1900. From a photograph in Orth, *op. cit.,* 752.

Figure 75. Case Hall, Cleveland, as completed in 1867, Heard and Blythe, architects. From a print in Payne, *op. cit.,* 44.

Figure 76. Case Hall, Cleveland, c. 1900. From a photograph in Orth, *op. cit.,* 474.

Figure 77. City Hall, Cleveland, erected in 1875. From a print in Payne, *op. cit.,* frontispiece.

Figure 78. Union Passenger Depot, Cleveland, c. 1900. From a photograph now in the Western Reserve Historical Society.

Figure 79. Forest City House, Cleveland, in 1876. From a print in Payne, *op. cit.,* 38.

Figure 80. Forest City House, Cleveland, c. 1880. From a photograph now in the Cleveland Public Library.

Figure 81. Ontario Street, east side, c. 1860. From a photograph in the Cleveland Public Library.

Figure 82. A. D. Herenden Building, Cleveland, erected in 1869. From a print in Payne, *op. cit.,* 172.

Figure 83. Brownell Street School, Cleveland, 1865. From a print in Payne, *op. cit.,* 80.

xii

Figure 84. Central High School, Cleveland, erected in 1856, Heard and Porter, architects. From a print in the Cleveland Public Library.

Figure 85. Central High School in 1900. From a photograph in the Cleveland Public Library.

Figure 86. St. Clair Street School, Cleveland, 1868, Heard and Blythe, architects. From a print in *Cleveland Public Schools. Thirty-third Annual Report of the Board of Education for the school year ending August 31, 1869. Cleveland. Fairbanks, 1870.* opp. p. 80.

Figure 87. Euclid Avenue Presbyterian Church, Cleveland 1853-59. From a photograph in the Western Reserve Historical Society.

Figure 88. Trinity Church, Cleveland, erected in 1854-5. Ingham, architect. From a photograph in the Western Reserve Historical Society.

Figure 89. Trinity Church, Cleveland, interior. From a photograph taken in 1890, now in the Cleveland Public Library.

Figure 90. Old Stone Church, Cleveland, erected in 1853-8, W. S. Warner, architect. Detail of a photograph of the Public Square, now in the Cleveland Public Library.

Figure 91. Old Stone Church, Cleveland, c. 1940. From a photograph in the Western Reserve Historical Society.

Figure 92. Second Baptist Church, Cleveland, erected in 1868-71. From a print in Payne, *op. cit.,* 150.

Figure 93. The Hurlburt House, Cleveland, erected 1855. Heard and Porter, architects. From a photograph in the Western Reserve Historical Society.

Figure 94. Amasa Stone House, Cleveland, erected in 1858. From a photograph in the Western Reserve Historical Society.

Figure 95. H. W. Kitchens House, Cleveland, erected in 1860. From a photograph in the Western Reserve Historical Society.

Figure 96. Rockefeller House, Cleveland, erected in 1868. From a photograph in the Cleveland Public Library.

Figure 97. O. D. Ford House, Cleveland, erected in 1874. From a print in *Atlas of Cuyahoga County,* 1876, 96.

INTRODUCTION

Within the past several decades the writing of architectural history has achieved new dimensions. Traditionally the historian has dealt with a group of important buildings chosen from the higher ranks in the architectural hierarchy. Major public and government buildings, churches and the residences of the elite were selected and the styles and periods of architectural history were drawn from their characteristics. The history of architecture was in fact the history of monuments in which vernacular design, utilitarian building and the work of the engineer had no part. Moreover, the attention of the scholar was centered almost entirely upon individual buildings, stylistically considered, while the environment in which each had its place was neglected. Each monument was lifted from its context and detached from its setting, and the history of architecture became at best a partial record of a few isolated symbols of cultural prestige.

The course of architectural development since the early 19th century has invalidated this traditional method. The democratic and technological revolutions and the process of urbanization are probably in large part responsible for the change. A new interest in folk art, the vernacular forms and the art of primitive peoples, all without traditional aristocratic standing, is one evidence of the change. The growing number of commercial and industrial buildings which make up our communities and demand recognition is certainly another. But beyond these factors, the domination of the urban center with its multiplicity of forms, its need for integration of functions and for a plan and a design which encompasses the total civic organism has forced a re-evaluation of architectural and planning practice. In these circumstances the significance of the individual building recedes, and the history of architecture, like architectural practice, becomes a study of larger units of which any given building is but one component. To place this component in its proper context is to relate it to the town as a whole and to the social and economic conditions to which it answers. The history of architecture then becomes the study of an urban complex and the individual building is thereby placed in perspective and endowed with three dimensions.

Though historians are engaged in rewriting the history of earlier periods in these terms, the 19th and 20th centuries are peculiarly susceptible to this treatment. The forces of mercantile and industrial expansion which distinguish this modern period have produced a civilization of urban centers, a metropolitan age, in which the significant new buildings and the vital planning activities center upon the city. As the term "environmental design" is increasingly being used to describe the integrated practice of city planner, landscape designer and architect, so modern architectural history might well be designated "environmental history."

This preoccupation with the total form of the city by designers and by historians has been forced upon us by the condition of our metropolitan centers. The symptoms of urban disease are many and flagrant. The several areas of the city are ill-adapted to their functions: industrial districts are congested and disorderly; commercial centers, usually concentrated at the center of town, have overbuilt the entire area, competing with one another for sun and air; residential streets are mechanical in pattern, and space for parks and recreational facilities have all but disappeared. Traffic overburdens the undifferentiated streets, mobility is reduced and the problems of parking and pedestrian safety become yearly more acute. Water and air pollution threatens the health and comfort of the populace.

The problems are found in their most aggravated form at the center of the city, a fact which arises from the history of the town. The central area is usually its oldest part, laid out in an age which could not anticipate mercantile and industrial development. The plan was calculated to serve a rural village of a few thousand people at most. For this purpose the arrangements were reasonable and efficient, but these rural conditions were of short duration. When commerce and industry were imposed upon this design, dislocation was inevitable. Here lies the root of the present urban difficulties. At this time when the very existence of the central city is threatened, and when strenuous efforts and enormous funds are being dedicated to its reincarnation, it is well to look attentively at the conditions and forces which produced the present chaos.

The factors here are utterly complex and, of course, vary from town to town. In these circumstances the only reasonable hope of clarity would appear to lie in the case study. Cleveland, Ohio, permits this necessary definition. By reason of its location and the period and character of its development, this city exemplifies the course taken by American cities as a whole in those early decades of the 19th century which underlie the present form of the town. Cleveland was founded in 1796 on an open site where complete freedom of design was possible. Its plan envisaged a small, rural community patterned after the New England village and by 1830 it had attained this projected form and measured up to the expectations of its founder.

This was, however, a temporary condition. After 1830 forces which had not been contemplated by the first designers came into being. Due to its location at the mouth of the Cuyahoga River where the Ohio-Erie Canal debouched upon the lake, it expanded rapidly in the period of canal and lake transportation. The balanced forms of the rural village were destroyed and the transformation to a mercantile city quickly consummated. The changes were pervading and sometimes destructive, and were no sooner accomplished than new forces were at work. The terrain of northern Ohio encouraged rapid extension of the railroads after mid-century and the confluence of Pennsylvania coal and Superior hematites at Cleveland produced an industrial city. Once again the character of the town was transformed and its problems multiplied. By 1875 the foundations of the modern city at its center were laid. The profound changes which were to revolutionize American society after the Civil War hardly affected the original design of the city. With the proverbial stubbornness of physical facts the form of the older parts of town resisted. Individual buildings were of course replaced, but until the recent major incisions directed by Planning Commissions, the central area of the city was confined to the strait-jacket created during the early decades of the 19th century.

This study, then, is concerned with the development of a characteristic American town in the first three-quarters of the 19th century. Two related things are involved: the design of the town as a whole; the terrain upon which it was laid; the tradition which directed the plan; and the many forces which shaped its growth. Secondly, there are the buildings which arose upon this plan: the skills and materials which shaped them; the styles from which they derived; and the many components of the culture which changed their character as the town prospered and developed. Together these constitute a physical environment in which the society of the time had its being, and which underlies the metropolis of the 20th century.

for survey. The Connecticut Land Company was thus organized, elaborate agreements were drawn up, intended to insure an equable division of the best lands, deeds were recorded at Hartford and later at Warren, Ohio, and a deed of trust executed.

In the spring of 1796 under the leadership of one of the directors of this Connecticut Land Company, Moses Cleaveland, a party was assembled at Schenectady. After an extremely arduous and occasionally hazardous trip, the surveying party arrived at the northeast corner of the present state of Ohio on July 4, 1796. Here the party was divided to facilitate the execution of their multiple commission: to survey that portion of the Reserve lying east of the Cuyahoga River into townships, to mark its boundaries, and to locate and lay out its principal town on an appropriate site.[2]

The first two parts of their task occupied the summer months, and by September 16, 1796, the surveyors were ready to lay out the town on the shore of the lake at the mouth of the Cuyahoga River.

The site was most advantageous. Here the narrow ribbon of the glaciated Erie Plain which skirted the lake to the east widened to form a deep triangle of level land. With its base on the lake and its apex imbedded eight miles deep in the receding plateau to the south this broad sweep of high, sandy shelf was bisected by the steep-sided valley of the Cuyahoga River. In the flat lands within the river valley the stream had left old abandoned beds and swampy spots, but on the table land on each side the ground was firm and well-drained. Against the sky-line the edges of the Portage escarpment gave definition to the site.

The several physiographic features which formed the state of Ohio met in this vicinity and their confluence, together with the glacial activity which had taken place in this region, prepared the site of the future city.[3] The heights which rise to the east and south of the site are the northern border of the Appalachian Plateau, terminated by the Portage Escarpment. The Erie Plain lies along the shore of the lake some eighty to one hundred feet above the present water level and west of the Cuyahoga it merges with the Central Lowland. The immediate foundations on which Cleveland was to be built were formed by the glaciers and their attendant lakes and rivers. The town was situated over a pre-glacial river bed which underlies the present ground level to a depth in places of over four hundred feet. This old valley, which had been much wider than the modern one, was filled with glacial deposits of clay, boulders and sand and was for a time the bottom of the series of glacial lakes preceding Lake Erie. Here the glacial river formed a delta where it entered the lakes, adding to the lake bottom a level strata of alluvial soil, sand and gravel. When the ice receded and the St. Lawrence exit far to the east was unblocked, the lake fell to its present level leaving the old delta standing some one hundred feet above the water. As the lake waters receded the Cuyahoga River worked through the easily cut gravels, carving out the present steep-sided valley, which with its tributary streams became significant in the layout and development of the future town.

Since the land west of the river was still occupied by the Indians in 1796, Moses Cleaveland chose the east bank for the site of his projected town. The first stage of the survey of this site was completed before the party left for the east in mid-October. It was carried out under the direction of Augustus Porter, the chief surveyor, and in all probability in large part was executed by Seth Pease, the second in command of the party. The results were recorded on the spot in the form of a rough sketch on pieces of foolscap pasted together and endorsed in the handwriting of still another member of the party, Amos Spafford: "Original Plan of the Town and Village of Cleaveland, Ohio, October 1st, 1796" (Figure 1)

The character of this original plan of Cleveland was to become a decisive factor in the development of the town.

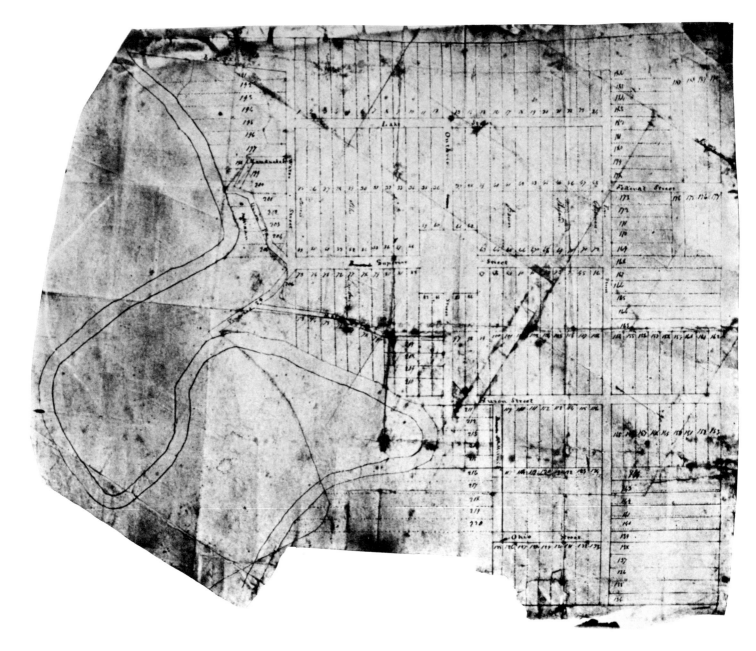

Its details are therefore of importance. This map laid down a ten-acre Public Square, bisected by two wide streets: Superior, one hundred and thirty-two feet wide, ran roughly east and west and Ontario which ran north and south was ninety feet wide. Using these as axes a large tract was described by four streets: Lake Street (Lakeside Avenue) on the north and Huron on the south; Water (West 9th) to the west near the river; Erie (East 9th) on the east. Together with Superior and Ontario these streets bounded four large oblongs, three of which were complete, but that on the south-west was truncated by the arm of the river and its steep bank. Four shorter streets served to extend the town east, south and west: Bath Street (vacated) along the lakeshore to the mouth of the river; Federal (St. Clair) extending east from a point between Lake and Superior; Miami (East 6th) and Ohio (Central Avenue) bounding a square to the south of Huron and west of Erie. These ten streets were the main thoroughfares of the projected town. Four narrower lanes served to connect the town to the river. Each was laid out at such an angle as to reduce the grade on the steep river bank. They converged in pairs on the two landings, one above and one below the giant loop in the river. On Spafford's map they were labelled Mandrake, Vineyard (Columbus Road), and Union Streets (West 10th), and Maiden Lane (vacated).

The tracts described by the main streets were divided into lots of two by ten chains, the rear of the lots meeting at a common median line which divided the tract in half. These lots were consequently regular in shape and two acres in extent. Adjacent to the lake and along the river banks, however, the lots varied in depth and were usually larger than those at the center of town. On the outskirts to the south and east, also, some of the lots were as much as four acres in extent. Two hundred and twenty-two lots were laid

Figure 1. First Plan of Cleveland, 1796.

out on this map of the city. Seth Pease made the official report on the survey of the town including survey notes and a copy, with minor changes, of Spafford's original map.

Such was the state of the survey of Cleveland when the party left for the east on October 17, 1796. A second party returned in 1797 and the work was continued under Seth Pease as principal surveyor, although a large part was actually carried out by Moses Warren. Beginning on August 20, 1797, he laid out three highways radiating to the east and south from the center of town. North Highway (St. Clair Avenue) roughly paralleled the lake shore and was an extension of Federal Street. Central Highway (Euclid Avenue) started from the east end of Huron Street and followed the mound marking the shore line of glacial Lake Warren, while South Highway (Kinsman Avenue) extended southwest from the south end of Erie Street. These roads were ninety-nine feet wide and separated from one another by angles of twenty-four degrees. Along both sides of each of them the so-called "outlots" or "ten-acre lots" were surveyed. The dividing lines between these ran at right angles to the roads they bordered and a median line between each pair of highways served as the common back line of the lots. Each lot was five chains wide on the street but inasmuch as the highways radiated, they increased in depth in proportion to the distance from town. Consequently they varied in size from ten acres near the city to forty acres on the east. Though Warren's notes on this survey were complete, no map was made of the ten-acre lots at this time.

In 1801 Spafford returned, re-surveyed the central area, marked the principal corners with oak posts and drew a new map. Several minor changes in the streets were made on this map and with these the principal features of the working plan of Cleveland were finally completed.

The arrangements made and completed by 1801 not only set the character of the pioneer village but in addition they became the framework about which the future city was to grow. During expansion virtually none of these original dispositions was erased. As the lots were purchased by settlers, privately-owned real estate values were created which had to be respected and the new streets, when required, were hence laid out along the dividing lines between lots.

At the center of town this resulted in subdivision of the oblong plots bounded by the ten main streets, which perpetuated the checkerboard design around the Public Square. To the south and east additional radiating streets were laid out along the rear lines common to the ten-acre lots, and the cross streets followed the lot-lines which ran at right angles to these highways. These were the stipulations inherent in the original plan and they were carried out so consistently that the outlines of the first plan may be traced in the streets of the city at its center to the present day. It is particularly true of Cleveland, then, that the first thoughts of the pioneer surveyors controlled the development of the city and the center of town today lives in large part within the framework of 1801. The adequacy of those first ideas is therefore of primary interest.

To determine how well or how ill the first surveyors planned it is essential to understand the problems which they faced. Though they had a virgin site at their disposal and their problems were to that extent simplified, the task of the surveyors was nonetheless sufficiently complicated. There were several factors to be considered and compromises to be made. The first was the matter of terrain. The contour of the land, the extent of the level stretches and the location and grade of declivities were inescapable determinants in the plan. Adjustments had to be made to them by the surveyors, but there were two equally important factors, namely, the traditional plan of a town as they knew it and the market value of the plots for speculative purposes.

As to terrain, they were presented with a comparatively level plateau, wedge-shaped and guarded by the steep banks of lake and river. This was an awkward circumstance for them inasmuch as the traditional plan to which they were committed was square and incompatible with the triangular site. To make it fit they laid out three tracts on as many quarters of the traditional square design and truncated the fourth. Together with other minor adjustments this compromise made possible the preservation of the familiar checkerboard plan on the irregular site, awkward though the results proved to be.

On the outskirts better adjustments were made. It was obvious that the river would play an important part in the life of the town; in fact the site was chosen in part because of the possibility of a future port. It was essential therefore that access be provided to the water. The four diagonal lanes were laid out to this end, following the terrain, and although one of them was quickly abandoned, it was soon replaced by Superior Lane which extended Superior Street to the river.[4] These lanes served their designated purpose for many years. Meantime on the east the radiating roads became increasingly important to the town. Central Highway, popularly designated as "the Buffalo Road," traversed the mound of the old shore-line of glacial Lake Warren and became the main route to the east through Doan's Corners. North Highway cut through a swamp along the lake shore at one point but was soon improved by drainage and fill, and South Highway became one of the thoroughfares to the southeast in later years. As the town expanded these three roads became important avenues within the city.

Though modifications were forced upon the surveyors by terrain, this was in fact the traditional way of laying out a town. It had been worked out as an ideal or norm intended to provide the spaces and relationships required in a small village. The open town center provided a focal point for town life and a central location for civic activities. It was used as a recreation area and a common pasture for livestock as well as a space for public buildings. The streets which bounded it were generously broad and straight, more than adequate for the carriage and horse traffic of the period. The square blocks which bordered the center gave to the town a neat and orderly, if somewhat mechanical appearance, and the lots were spacious enough for gardens around each house. The many corner sites were taken up, as the town grew, by stores and hotels. Beyond the center of town larger plots were used for farming and pasturing within walking distance, and the radiating roads led across country to neighboring villages. It was an orderly, competent arrangement which was quite adequate until commerce and industry changed the whole conception of the functions of a town.

The fact is that by reason of their New England background and surveying experience there and in New York State these men knew no other way to lay out a town. It was their every intention to reproduce in the wilderness of the Western Reserve another such village as they had left in the east. In fact, great pride was repeatedly expressed, as Cleveland developed, in its close resemblance to the towns of Connecticut.[5] That this plan for a rural agricultural community would soon be overwhelmed by commerce and industry, could hardly, in 1796, have been anticipated.

Meantime another compelling motive influenced the design as originally conceived by the surveyors. Virtually the whole area now within the state of Ohio was developed by land companies and the opening of the Western Reserve and the establishment of Cleveland were parts of this process. The Connecticut Land Company had no genuine interest in either of them beyond the sale of the land, and the surveys were hence calculated primarily to serve the ends of real estate speculation. The system of land survey, invented in the eighteenth century and used by Seth Pease and his assistants in the summer of 1796 to lay out the Reserve, was designed to facilitate sales. It divided the country into equal plots regardless of terrain so that they might be marketed at standard prices.[6] In this manner the less desirable tracts would be taken up along with contiguous valuable ones. By standardizing in this manner, the work of survey was reduced, the sale of plots simplified and the possibilities of litigation minimized.

Although this regular division of the land best served all purposes in the countryside, some further efforts to equalize values were commonly used in the towns. Since the town plots would presumably become quite valuable, an effort was made to compensate for inequalities due to terrain or location. The less desirable sites were increased in size so that they would not be neglected by purchasers. In the case of Cleveland all the lots bordering on the main streets were a regular two acres in extent, but on the edges of the village to the east and south where land values could not be expected to rise so rapidly, some of the lots were as much as double this size. On the steep slopes next to the river and lake a large number of marginal lots, considerably less desirable as building sites, were also larger. Then, too, the outlots were designed between radiating roads, so the penalty of distance had compensation in size. These were clearly adjustments intended to attract buyers.

Some thought was nonetheless given to the future prosperity and usefulness of the town as an organism. The plan of sale proposed by the head surveyor, Augustus Porter, is of some interest. He suggested that all lots fronting on the Square be reserved for public purposes, together with portions of the "flats" along the river as thought advisable.[7] These reservations would have preserved the civic center and parts of the river front for public use, greatly to the benefit of the future city. It would not be many years before the dire need for such reserved areas would be felt. His plans, however, were not adopted, much to the later detriment of the city.

From the vantage point of the present it is clear that a great opportunity was missed in this design. The surveyors, of course, had no interest in creating anything new in the wilderness. Their duty was done when a paper chart was prepared, the survey notes completed, and a few corners were marked by oak posts. Their whole training led them to create a conventional design and so, presented with the boundless opportunity of an untrammeled site, they laid down the mechanical plan dictated by tradition, modifying it in the face of insistent terrain conditions by a few improvisations. They were under orders to meet the demands of a speculative real estate operation and they further compromised their plan to carry out those orders. This dual influence of tradition and selfish economic interest was to have a long history in the future of Cleveland.

The "town" on the high eastern bank at the mouth of the Cuyahoga River remained for several years little more than a chart drawn from survey notes. On the site itself, the only evidences of a settlement seem to have been a number of oak posts buried in a dense forest, a scattering of log cabins on the side hill or atop the bank above the river, and a woods road or two where wide avenues had been planned. Only gradually over the years, as the population slowly increased, were the ten main streets and the Public Square to emerge one at a time from the forest.

Many things militated against the rapid growth of the village. The journey from the east was one of extreme difficulty and few were willing to undertake it. No roads led to these northern shores until 1798, and the "Girdled Road" which was then cut through from the Pennsylvania border was at first little more than a woods trail. It was ungraded and unbridged at the streams, filled with brush and blocked by stumps and fallen timber and was for some time virtually impassible to the Conestoga wagons on which the traveller depended to transport his household goods. Connections with the Ohio valley to the south, where the water highway encouraged immigration, were no better. Until the second decade of the century, the only route available was the Portage Path, an Indian trail unfit for wheeled traffic.[8] Under these conditions the number of settlers who ventured into northern Ohio were few indeed compared to the stream of immigrants along the Ohio River.

There was, moreover, little enough incentive, once the arduous journey from the east had been undertaken, to proceed all the way to the Cuyahoga River. In the early years of the 19th century there was no real town on this site to add amenities to the hardships of pioneer life. A living could be made from the land just as easily farther east, and land was immeasurably cheaper in the back country. In these conditions, most of the pioneers stopped before they reached the prospective town. The eastern part of the Reserve was rapidly growing in population while Cleveland still consisted of a few scattered cabins, and Cuyahoga County had a population of 1500 when that of Cleveland was 57 in the year 1810.[9]

The hardships of the frontier were at their worst in Cleveland. Despite the open appearance of the paper plan, the actual site was virtually an unbroken forest. Unlike the shores of the Ohio River, there were no spaces ready for cultivation. Every foot of ground had to be freed of trees by the laborious process of cutting, burning and grubbing out stumps before the land could be planted or a cabin built. Several decades were to pass before even the main streets were freed of stumps and the forest pushed back from the center of town.

As if these accumulated difficulties were not sufficient, a final, unpredictable hardship was visited upon the early settlers. They suffered from that most serious plague of pioneer life, "ague and fever." This disease was characterized by alternate chills and fever, often accompanied by nausea, which attacked whole families for weeks at a time.

Figure 2. Mouth of the Cuyahoga River in 1800.

It was sometimes so devastating as to leave no one in the household well enough to supply the sick with food, much less carry on the hard labors of frontier life. This affliction nearly depopulated the town in 1798 and 1799. It was attributed to the "miasmal conditions" which arose from the swampy land at the river mouth, and most of the pioneers left the vicinity for the higher land on the ridges to the south or east. Of the some forty-odd people who arrived during the last years of the century, only seven were left in the town by 1800, while a much larger number lived on its outskirts.[10]

Despite these deterrents, the possibility of future prosperity in the town itself continued to attract the hardier immigrants and the population gradually rose. The threat of the British on Lake Erie frightened away many during the war of 1812, and conscription of the young men worked further hardship on the little community. But these were temporary discouragements and by 1815, almost twenty years after its founding, there were thirty-four houses and a population of some 150 persons in the village.[11]

No pictorial record of the appearance of Cleveland in 1815 exists. Several drawings of the mouth of the Cuyahoga River, made from memory at a later date, are the only visual records in the first years of the 19th century (Figure 2). Quite a large number of pen descriptions, however, are extant, thanks largely to the activities of the *Early Settler's Association of Cuyahoga County*.[12] Some of these are graphic enough to convey a picture of the town in the years just prior to 1815. I. A. Morgan, who lived south of town, leaves this record:[13]

> My first distinct recollection of Cleveland dates back to 1812, when I rode behind my father on horseback to Cleveland, which possibly, then contained twenty families . . . . Then there were many large stumps in the Square, and clumps of bushes which extended to the lake, and all along the bank of the lake, from

the summit to the beach, the trees were all standing . . . . On the south side of Superior Street, from the Square to near where the American House now is, was woods, except some four or five spaces adjoining the street for as many houses and gardens. Where Prospect Street is now, next to Ontario, was the old cemetery, west, south and east, the forest stood in its native grandeur. Only a narrow strip had been cut out for a road where Ontario Street is.

Samuel Williamson, whose father had arrived in Cleveland in 1810, was about five years old at the time he first remembers the town. He states:[14]

> I will say that at my earliest recollection Water Street had been opened; that is, the timber had been cut out and a wagon road was run through the center of the street from Superior to Bank [sic], . . . It had all grown up, however, with elder bushes, thick all the way along. There were occasional trees and some houses upon it. The house nearest the lake was that of Alfred Kelley . . . and was the first brick house built in this city. It stood upon the corner of Water and Bank [sic] . . . . On Superior Street it was cleared of timber, so far as I remember, up to the Public Square, and the Public Square partly. The old court house stood on the northwest corner of the square. The street was full of large stumps, but otherwise than that it was clear. There were quite a number of houses . . . . Going south on Ontario Street there was a wagon track until you reached where Mr. Walworth owned. There was an opening there extending down the hill, and that was the only clearing there was for some distance in that direction.

Further evidence of the town's appearance is suggested by I. A. Morgan's list of its residents and their home sites somewhat earlier, in 1811:[15]

> Farther down toward the square from the south came Judge John Walworth, then postmaster, and his oldest son, A. W. Walworth, and son-in-law, Dr. David Long. Then on the corner where the Forest City House now stands [West

Figure 3. Plan of Cleveland, 1814.

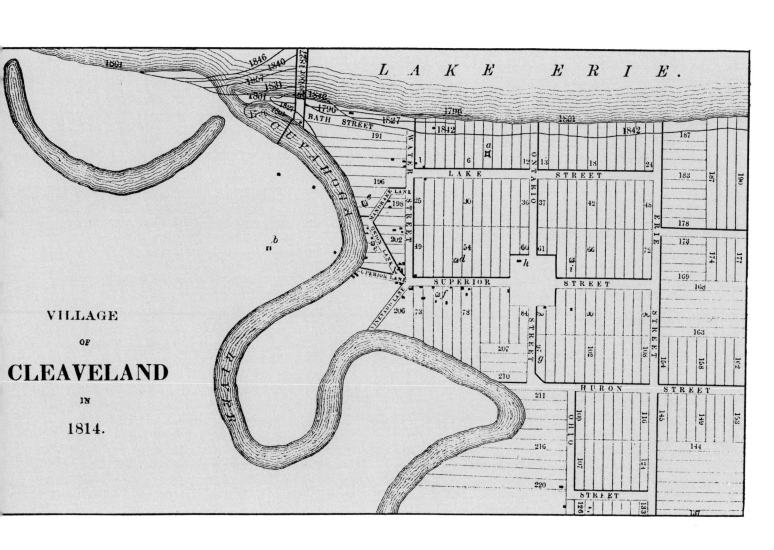

LAKE ERIE.

VILLAGE
OF
CLEAVELAND
IN
1814.

Superior at the Public Square], was a Mr. Morey. The next was near the American House [the south side of Superior nearly opposite the end of East 6th Street], where the little post office then stood, occupied by Mr. Hanchet, who had just started a little store. Close by was a tavern kept by Mr. George Wallace. On the top of the hill north of Main Street [Superior], Lorenzo Carter and son, Lorenzo, Jr., who kept tavern also. The only house below on Water Street was owned by Judge Samuel Williamson, with his family and his brother Mathew, who had a tannery on the side hill below. On the corner of Water and Superior Streets was Nathan Perry's store, and his brother, Horace Perry, lived near by.

Morgan goes on to give an itemized list of the residents of the outlying districts, at Doan's Corners four miles to the east, on the ridge south of town, and at Newburgh, a settlement some seven miles inland. The effects of the "ague" were still being felt in Cleveland, and this list is notably longer than that for the city itself.

In 1814 Alfred Kelley whose pretentious house is referred to by Williamson, made a copy of Spafford's map of the 1801 survey on which he noted the extant buildings (Figure 3). He places a group of houses on the south side of Superior, which are widely spaced, as indicated in the descriptions, and in some cases placed deep in the lots. Two smaller groups are gathered on Water Street at its intersections with Superior and with Lake, while a few lie in between on the side-hill. A lonely house or two lie deep in the forest south of the Square.

In the neighborhood of 1815 then, Cleveland consisted of two main streets, Superior and Water. Both of these had been cleared of trees to their full width, but stumps remained, and bushes grew undisturbed in the open space. A narrow track was used for traffic down their centers. Ontario was open only south of the Square, and even there it was no more than a woods road. The Square was half-forest-ed, and its cleared area was still filled with stumps. The scattered houses on Superior and Water Streets were set in small clearings, separated one from another by uncut forest. A few small stores, a tannery, and several public houses constituted the commercial activity of the town.

At this stage in the town's development, its inhabitants were far too occupied with the back-breaking tasks of clearing the land and maintaining themselves in the face of the rigors of the pioneer life to be concerned with appearances. Their dwellings were those which could be constructed most easily and with the least waste of time. Log cabins which required less work and also considerably less skill than the frame houses they had known in New England could be quickly erected, using the logs which the builder had, in any case, to cut in order to clear his land. Most of them were certainly very modest, consisting of one or perhaps two rooms, and they were usually confined to one floor. The logs used were some sixteen to eighteen feet in length and were notched near the ends so as to lock together at the corners. The cracks between logs were stuffed with moss, and windows were frequently omitted. The door was narrow and often closed by a blanket. The chimney consisted of crossed logs, fire-proofed by clay. Window glass was a luxury and the floor might well be packed earth at first, though as soon as possible a "puncheon" floor would be laid. The roof consisted of split "shakes," until time could be found for the laborious task of splitting out shingles.[16]

This was a rude dwelling at best and the pioneer aspired to a more pretentious one as soon as the pressures of establishing himself on the frontier permitted. Houses, warehouses and stores of logs continued to be built for over a decade, however, and many still stood as late as 1825. Even when sawn lumber became available, a hybrid building was sometimes built, the structure of which was of logs and the facing of board. One such was the second cabin built by Lorenzo Carter in 1803 which is described by Kelley in the paragraphs below. Though of logs, it was covered with boards to simulate a frame house.[17] But in the midst of the wilderness, the pioneer longed for the amenities of life, and the amenities meant the ways of the New England village. As in the case of the town plan, so in the case of his buildings, he intended to reproduce his eastern surroundings in the new location. The method of house framing which he already knew was put to use as soon as conditions permitted. Since a far greater degree of skill was required than for a log cabin, the first such buildings of record were built by carpenters. Samuel Dodge, who arrived in 1798, was the earliest. In 1801 he erected a frame barn for Samuel Huntington.[18] A second trained artisan, Levi Johnson, built the first dwelling to be constructed in this manner in 1809.[19] The first frame store was that of Elias and Harvey Murray, which dates from the same season.[20] It seems that the first attempt at such a large scale building as a warehouse was not made until 1817, when one of frame construction was raised by Case and Gaylord.[21]

By 1810 the log-cabin village was being invaded by these frame structures. According to Alfred Kelley:[22]

> Cleveland city in 1810 contained three framed dwelling houses and some five or six log houses. Of the three frame dwellings, one (that of Judge Nathan Perry) on the corner of Superior and Water Streets was of two stories, — that occupied by George Wallace on the corner of Superior Street and Vineyard Lane, as a tavern, was one and a half stories, and that of Samuel Williamson (afterwards Judge Williamson) on the W. side of Water Street near St. Clair Street was of one story. Neither of these houses was finished. Of the log houses that of Major Lorenzo Carter, standing on top of the bank near the N.W. corner of Superior Street was by far the largest. It was of two low stories — weather boarded so as to have the appearance on the outside, of a frame house.

The type of frame houses here indicated could be built with hand tools, although at the cost of a good deal of hard labor and time. Such tools as were required — a broad-axe, saws, bits, chisels, and hammers — were the standard equip-

ment of the carpenter and could be brought in the kit of the immigrant. The method of construction was the usual one employed at the same period in the east. The corner posts, sills, plates and summer beams were usually hand hewn with a broad-axe. The corner braces and smaller floor beams were sawn, if possible, and the clapboard siding was sawn. Shingles for roofs and walls, when so used, were split. The joints were made by drilling the mortise for the tenon and squaring the holes with chisels. Pins of oak thrust through drilled holes fastened the members tightly in place. Few nails were required, and these were small ones used to attach the siding or shingles. The following description by a Cleveland resident is pertinent:[23]

> Half a century ago [c. 1835] men built houses which they intended should be substantial, though they were not always elegant. When the timbers had been hewed, it took from thirty to forty men to raise the house. It took two strong men to hold the foot of the post . . . . The whole building was put together with huge wooden pins.

No pictorical record and no adequate description of these first frame buildings exist. For the Court House of Cuyahoga County, however, both are available. It was located on the northwest corner of the Public Square, and was so indicated on the map by Alfred Kelley in 1814. It was built under contract from the county commissioners in 1812-1813 by Levi Johnson who was responsible for many of the most ambitious projects of the period.[24] He frequently proved that he had the proverbial ingenuity of the pioneer in solving problems of construction, and in the case of the Court House, he produced a unique building.[25] It was about twenty-five by fifty feet on plan and two stories in height. Half of the lower floor consisted of a two-cell jail at one end. This part of the building was constructed of squared logs some three feet in length, placed transversely and bolted together so that they formed an unbreachable wall. The rest

of the building was ordinary frame construction. On the ground floor, living quarters for the jailor were provided adjacent to the cells, and on the second a single large hall. This large upper room served a multiplicity of uses. It was used for social gatherings, and town meetings, for religious services and lectures, and as a court room when occasion demanded. It thus became the first civic center of the infant community. The exterior of the building, including the uniquely constructed jail, was covered with clap-board and painted red. Its severely plain and solid appearance may be judged by a water color made in 1875 from a drawing composed by one who was familiar with the original building (Figure 4). This shows a simple, oblong building, four-square and without adornment of any kind. Its windows and doors are framed by flat boards apparently painted white against the red, clap-board walls. No mouldings nor ornamental carving interrupt the plain, flat surfaces. It is apparent that for all his ingenuity in construction, Levi Johnson was no architect, and that the frontier community was not yet prepared to reproduce the fine proportions and refined craftsmanship of the East. If this degree of simplicity was found in the most important building in the village, it is probable that the private houses were simpler still.

After almost two decades of struggle the community of Cleveland was still a very primitive place. In the face of discouraging hardships of travel and land clearing, and despite the setbacks due to war and disease, it now could claim some thirty-odd houses and a population of about 150 people. Its two streets were still full of stumps and the Public Square was only half cleared. Its buildings were mostly log cabins of primitive construction, but frame buildings were commencing to appear even though they were very simple in form, and it boasted two structures of brick. The patches of cleared land were being widened and the town was beginning to take form as a village. Warehouses on the river and stores on the main streets housed a few rudimentary commercial activities. Despite its frontier character, Cleveland in 1815 was on the brink of a period of rapid development and increasing prosperity.

Figure 4. First Court House, 1812-1813.

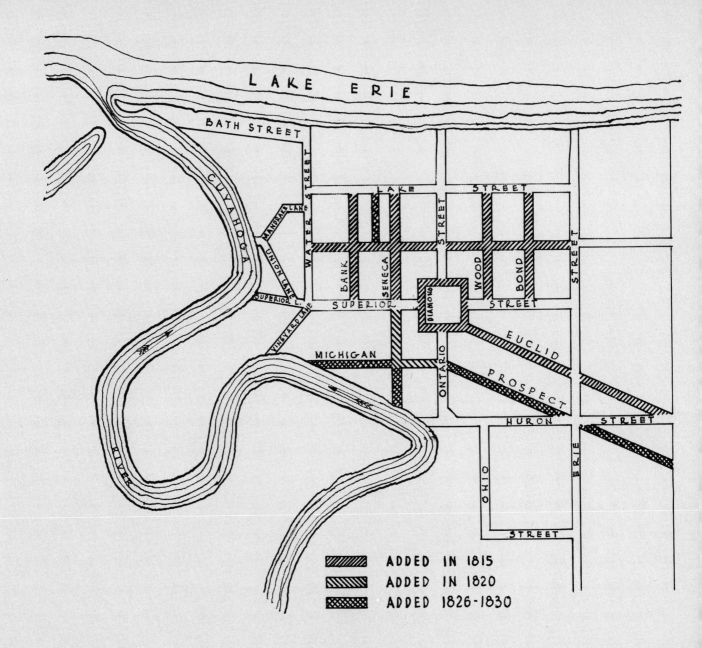

LAKE ERIE

BATH STREET

CUYAHOGA

RIVER

WATER STREET

MANDRAKE LANE
UNION LANE
SUPERIOR L.
VINEYARD LANE

BANK
SENECA

LAKE STREET

SUPERIOR

DIAMOND

WOOD
BOND

STREET

STREET

STREET

EUCLID

PROSPECT

MICHIGAN

ONTARIO

HURON STREET

ERIE

OHIO

STREET

▨▨▨ ADDED IN 1815
▨▨▨ ADDED IN 1820
▨▨▨ ADDED 1826-1830

CHAPTER TWO

THE NEW ENGLAND VILLAGE 1815-1830

The decade and a half, from 1815 to 1830, was a period in the development of Cleveland during which it gradually lost the character of a pioneer community and assumed, one step at a time, the appearance and attributes of a small New England village. Due in large measure to improved transportation facilities, including new roads and the gradual improvement of old ones, bridges over the river, steam craft on the Lake, harbor improvements at the mouth of the river, and finally the canals, the town increased rapidly in size and population. Ground clearing operations were extended, new streets were laid out, and the buildings took on an architectural dignity impossible up to this time. The village was incorporated and its limits extended. Newspapers came into being along with a bookstore and a forum, and finally the first church and school, together with a new courthouse and several hotels were built. By the time the effects of the canals reached Cleveland in the late 1820's, it had attained the form of its New England prototypes, an open and well-balanced village. In 1830 few traces remained of the primitive frontier community.

The first stimulation was provided by the construction of roads connecting Cleveland with Wooster and with the Ohio

Figure 5. Street Development of Cleveland, 1815-1830.

River shortly after the war of 1812. Thereafter Cleveland was no longer an isolated outpost. Immigrants and goods arrived more freely, if at first in relatively small volume, which "gave to the prosperity of Cleveland a decided impetus," to quote Alfred Kelley's letter to John Bar. Certainly these roads must have been primitive enough, mostly ungraded, filled with mudholes in wet weather or with iron-hard ruts in the clay soil when dry. But passage was now possible, no matter how slow and uncomfortable, and the town responded. A mail coach route was established with regular deliveries between Cleveland and Painesville to the east in 1818. In 1820 a line of stages traveled between Cleveland and Columbus and a second line connected Cleveland and Norwalk. In 1821 two new routes brought the east nearer to the frontier when both Pittsburgh and Buffalo were linked to Cleveland by stage.[26] Meantime the extension of the National Road from Wheeling to Zanesville in 1825 greatly stimulated trade and immigration in southern Ohio and with her new connections to the south, Cleveland likewise benefited.[27] At Cleveland itself an important sign of prosperity was the construction of bridges to supplement the little ferry which was the only means of crossing the river before 1822. The *Cleveland Leader* states on June 6th of that year:

Public spirited individuals have liberally undertaken to erect two permanent, well-made Free Bridges across the Cuyahoga River, at a distance of a half-mile from each other. They are begun and sufficient means are furnished for their completion during the present season.

The hazards of Lake travel were simultaneously reduced. In 1818 the first steamboat on Lake Erie reached Cleveland. The famous Walk-in-the-Water, small and primitive as it was, opened an era of water traffic which was to assure the prosperity of the lake port at the Cuyahoga River. It was soon clear that if Cleveland were to benefit properly from the increased lake traffic, the sand bar across the mouth of the river would have to be removed and the harbor dredged to accommodate ships of considerable draft. After much agitation and the laying of many abortive plans, the first concrete step was taken in this direction in 1825. Five thousand dollars was appropriated by the Federal Government for work on the Cleveland harbor and a pier was built from the east shore of the river. This failed to create an open channel, however, and a second and larger appropriation was made. With this a second pier was built to the east of the first and the channel was changed to flow between the two. By 1828, dredging had provided ten feet of water in the channel and the harbor was a success.[28] In conjunction with these harbor improvements, the opening of the canal from the Ohio River to Cleveland in 1827 was the foundation for a new era in the life of the town.

Meantime as early as 1814 the forward-looking members of the small community anticipated the coming expansion. On December 23, 1814, the village was incorporated.[29] The articles of incorporation described the village as so much of the city plat as lay north of Huron Street and west of Erie as originally laid out by the Connecticut Land Company.[30] On October 15, 1815, the town council met to lay out a number of streets.

Though only two of the original ten streets had been cleared by 1815, and were flanked at intervals by houses, the commission now laid out six new ones (Figure 5). Most of these were surveyed through a still dense forest and would not be used, in some cases, for many years. These streets were, first, four lying between the original north-south streets from Superior to the lake, namely, Bank (West 6th), Seneca (West 3rd), Wood (East 3rd), and Bond (East 6th).[31] These divided the two original large plots of ground north of the square into three parts each and were laid out on the division lines between lots. Secondly, Federal Street (St. Clair) was extended westward to the river along the rear lines of the lots fronting on Superior and Lake Streets. This served to bisect those same tracts laterally. Since Federal Street, as originally surveyed, did not lie exactly halfway between Lake and Superior, this entailed a jog at Erie (East 9th) to preserve the integrity of the lots in these blocks. In the third place, streets describing the periphery of the Public Square were laid out and called collectively Diamond Street. Finally a radical departure from the traditional gridiron plan was designed at this time. Central Highway (Euclid Avenue) was cut through from its terminus at Huron Street to the southeast corner of the Public Square. Though still just a woods road, it was apparent that Central Highway would become in the next years an important route from the east and plans for its early development were wisely laid at this time. This diagonal street cutting across expensive lots, marks a turning point in the development of the town which was to bear important fruit in the expansion of the plan within a few years.

As the town continued to increase in population during the Twenties many new streets were added. In 1820 the village council extended Seneca Street south of Superior and drew Michigan (now obliterated) to intersect it at right angles. The area so defined balanced exactly the corresponding block north of Superior bounded by Seneca and Federal, preserving the checkerboard in this sector of the village.[32]

This many of the new streets were created by the town council. After 1826, however, the citizens themselves appear to have had a hand in initiating the opening of new streets and alleys. Between 1826 and 1830, a dozen notices of petition to the council for a new street appear in the newspapers. On January 6, 1826, this typical item is found in the *Cleaveland Herald*:

> Notice. A petition will be presented to the Board of Trustees of the City of Cleaveland on the 20th day of February next, praying said Board to lay out and continue Seneca Street on its southwardly termination and intersection with Michigan Street to the Cuyahoga River. Cleaveland, Dec. 30, 1825.

This petition apparently bore fruit, for on the map of Cleveland of 1835 Seneca appears so extended to the river. But by no means all such petitions met with success. Nine petitions involving eleven streets or alleys found their way into the newspapers by 1830, and of these only four received favorable action. In addition to the extension of Seneca, a petition appeared in the *Herald* on September 8, 1826, for an alley between Seneca and Bank from St. Clair to Lake; "... on the line between village lots 30 and 31 and running northerly on the line of said lots ...," thus preserving the lot values, and the geometry of this part of town. In the next year a petition, once again appearing in the *Herald*, to continue Michigan Street westward from Seneca to the canal basin was approved.

Of these the fourth petition acted upon favorably was of most interest. It proposed a diagonal street paralleling Central Highway one block to the south. The latter had been, of course, a main road which approached the village from beyond its boundaries. But here, for the first time, a city street which lay entirely within the borders of the village was designed to cut across lots diagonally. With this precedent additional radiating streets were laid out toward the east and south after 1830, many of which have since become the main arteries of transportation in the expanding city. This first diagonal way was named Prospect Street and was in a real sense, a turning point in the conception of the village design. As will be seen in a later chapter, the regular block and the right-angled crossing were by no means abandoned, but the new diagonal thoroughfare was now added as a supplement to the gridiron plan.

The first actual enlargement of the village limits was made in 1829. In that year the state legislature permitted the town of Cleveland to include a small section along the river near Huron Street within its jurisdiction[33] (B, Figure 6).

All of this expansion was, of course, in response to the increasing population. These figures on population are given by Whittlesey: in 1820 there were about 150 people; in 1825, 500 people; and in 1830 there were 1075 in the town. Thus in a decade the population multiplied seven times.

To accommodate this increase, rapid progress was made in clearing the ground of forest. The method employed was recorded in a description of a "bee" of somewhat later date by an early resident:[34]

> I will tell you of the bee on my father's farm .... The men were assembled; they were divided up into two parties, and each party had a yoke of oxen. One drove, one carried the log chain and four or five rolled logs together. The piles were about ten feet high and about the same width and from twelve to sixteen feet long. In one day from forty to fifty log heaps were made .... There was little market for wood, but such trees as were thought suitable had been drawn away and cut and split for firewood by the boys. When the men had finished their work the fun began. About sunset the boys and girls set fire to the heaps. It was dry season and the flames leaped and darted over the dry wood and an immense conflagration was soon well under way.

This profligate waste was typical of the practice throughout this region in the settling period. The superb forest cover was little more than a nuisance to the pioneers. It was, of

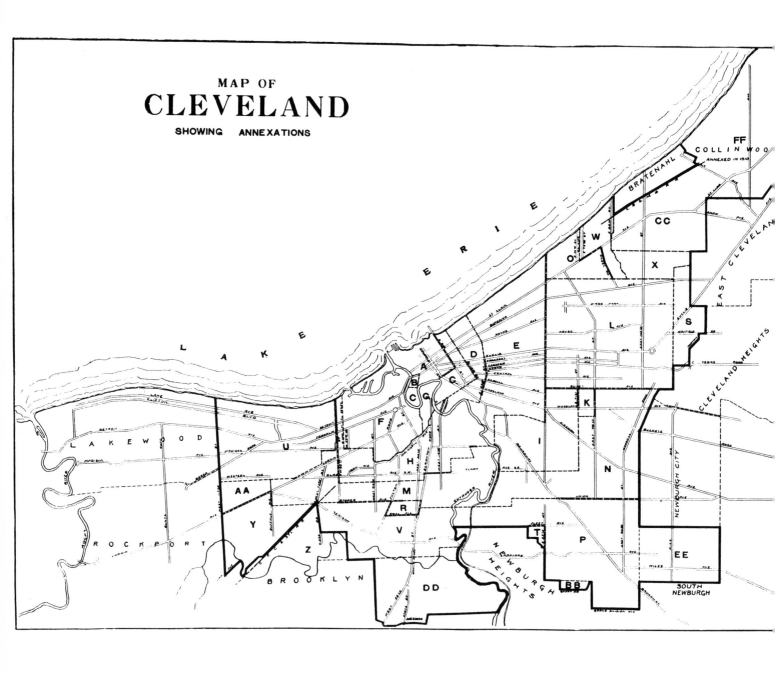

MAP OF
CLEVELAND
SHOWING ANNEXATIONS

K E Y

A Incorporated as Village of Cleveland 12/23/1814.

B Annexed to Village of Cleveland by act of General Assembly 12/1/1829.

C Annexed to Village of Cleveland by act of General Assembly 12/19/1834.

D Incorporated with A. B. and C. as City of Cleveland 3/5/1836.

E Ten-acre lots annexed to City of Cleveland 3/22/1850.

F City of Ohio annexed 5/5/1854. F. was incorporated as City of Ohio 3/3/1836.

G Part of Brooklyn Township annexed 2/20/1867.

H I Parts of Brooklyn and Newburgh Townships annexed 2/20/1867.

K Part of Newburgh Township 100 A lot No. 333 annexed 12/14/1869.

L East Cleveland Village annexed 10/24/1872.

M N O Parts of Brooklyn, Newburgh, and East Cleveland Townships annexed 11/19/1872.

P Part of Newburgh Township annexed 9/16/1873.

R Part of Brooklyn Village annexed 11/10/1890.

S Part of East Cleveland Township annexed 6/27/1892.

T Part of Newburg Township, part of original lot 312 annexed 2/12/1894.

U West Cleveland Village annexed 3/5/1894.

V Brooklyn Village annexed 4/30/1894.

W Glenville Village annexed 9/26/1898.

X Glenville Village, second ward, annexed 12/20/1902.

Y Linndale Village annexed 4/11/1904.

Z Part of Brooklyn Village annexed 4/11/1904. Reconsidered and lost, 6/31/1904.

A A Part of Brooklyn Township annexed 1/11/1904.

B B Part of Newburgh Heights Village annexed 9/25/1905.

C C City of Glenville annexed 6/19/1905.

D D Village of Saith Brooklyn annexed 12/11/1905.

E E Village of Corbett, annexed.

F F Village of Collinwood annexed January, 1910.

course, used for building and for fuel, but it was a serious hindrance to cultivation and to the opening of town lots and streets. The chief interest of the settlers lay in getting rid of the trees as efficiently as possible, so they cut and burned on a grand scale.

The period from 1815 to 1830 is the most difficult one in which to visualize the appearance of the town. The descriptions in the *Annals of the Early Settler's Association* are quite naturally concerned primarily with the very earliest recollections. The first newspapers contained little local news, much less descriptions of what all their readers could see with their own eyes. No drawings nor prints of the town proper exist which date before 1833.

One graphic description from the *Annals* is of interest, however. In September of 1824, Harvey Rice, who was destined to become one of Cleveland's early historians, arrived and described his first impressions thus:[35]

> In the morning I took a stroll to see the town and in less than half an hour saw all there was of it. The town even then was proud of itself and called itself the "gem of the west." In fact the Public Square was begemmed with stumps, while near its center glowed its crowning jewel, a log [sic] courthouse. The eastern border of the Square was skirted by the native forest which abounded in rabbits and squirrels and afforded the villagers a "happy hunting ground." The entire population did not exceed four hundred souls. The dwellings were generally small but were interspersed here and there with pretentious mansions.

By adding the few clues offered by such descriptions to the record of new streets laid out in the decade and one half after 1815 one may visualize the expansion of the town thus: the northwest quadrant of the original plan was the first area to be cleared and built up. By 1820 this district was sufficiently populated so that the block to the south of Superior was invaded, a fact made evident by the extension of

Seneca and the design of Michigan Street in this quadrant. By 1830 eastward expansion was indicated by the Prospect Street development. In sum, the village first filled out the northwest block between the Public Square and the river. During the 1820's it extended southward across Superior Street and at the end of this period had begun to penetrate the area across Ontario Street to the east.

During this same period a certain degree of specialization of areas within the town became apparent. Aided by the harbor improvements between 1825 and 1830, which included piers on either side of a dredged channel, a deepened harbor and bridges across the river, the banks of the stream between the mouth of the river and Superior Lane became a wholesale and warehouse district. This section on the flats was connected to the town above by numerous roads. At the mouth of the river, Bath Street led to Water Street above. Upstream three lanes, Mandrake, St. Clair and Union, converged on the landing below St. Clair Street. At the first bend in the river Superior Lane, recently installed, gave access to the main street of town.

Superior Street was the center of the retail business section. The private houses which first lined this wide street were taken over one at a time by stores and hotels. Merwin's Mansion House, the earliest hotel of any size, was located at the juncture of Superior and Vineyard Lane. In 1820 a second hotel, the Cleveland House, was built at the other end of Superior at the Square. Between them, the most affluent hotel yet seen was erected by Philo Scovill and named the Franklin House in 1825. Throughout the length of Superior the number of retail establishments increased each year as more goods became available with the improvement of transportation facilities.

Between Superior and Lake and from Ontario to the river, the block subdivided in 1815 gradually became the most important residential district in town. Alfred Kelley's brick house near Water and Lake was the most pretentious and formed the nucleus for a colony of log and frame dwellings. That this was the residential center of town is also demonstrated by the fact that at the center of this area both the first and second schools were located and Trinity Church, the first in the village, was placed nearby in 1828.

In the 1820's Public Square also began to receive more attention. Around its periphery several of the finest residences were built as outposts to the concentration of private dwellings to the northwest. Included among these was that of Leonard Case on the north side of Superior at the eastern edge of the Public Square, built in 1824, and Lemen House directly across Superior Street in 1829. Meantime the old red painted log and clapboard Court House was replaced by an imposing new one of brick and stone in 1828. Some thought was given at the same time to the landscaping of this civic center. No sooner had the stumps been cleared from the Square and the main streets than it became necessary to replace the trees so profligately cut to clear the ground. Ara Sprague states:[36] "In the spring of 1827, I helped set out the first shade trees on the north side of the park [Square]."

Along with this physical progress, there were numerous other indications that the pioneer period was nearing its close. In 1818 the first newspaper appeared. This was the *Gazette and Commercial Register*, a weekly sheet which consisted largely of stories for the entertainment of its readers and a few items of news of national importance. In the next year the enterprising *Cleveland Herald* entered the field and soon eclipsed the pioneer *Gazette*. In 1825 the *Herald* was enlarged and took on local advertising and news, and rapidly attained importance in the community. As the frontier aspect of the town faded, the need of intellectual outlets became felt. The first local forums were organized in 1820 and a book store was established in the same year. Meantime the first formal school with its own building came into being in 1817 with the erection of the small frame schoolhouse on St. Clair between Bank and Seneca. This was quickly outgrown and a more spacious Academy was constructed across the street in 1821. The first church building was not built, however, until 1828 when Trinity was erected in the same neighborhood.

The combination of rapid growth of population and lateral expansion of the village created an unprecedented demand for new buildings during these years, and at the same time, as the village attained stability and aspired to greater dignity, architectural forms of better quality were required. An increased supply of building materials and a larger number of skilled builders were now needed. Both needs were met with the same energy which characterized the village in other respects during these decades. Wood was naturally the principal building material. Much of this was available on the site as the land was gradually cleared. These trees were mostly hardwoods, suitable for the massive frames of the buildings and were in good supply for this purpose. But pine lumber was preferred for siding since it was more easily shaped and handled and importations from Canada were made at an early date. Witness these advertisements in the *Cleveland Herald* in 1826:

30,000 feet of first rate Pine lumber just received from Canada, and for sale wholesale and retail, at the wharf, by J. H. Guptil, Cleaveland.

Also:

Ten thousand feet of pine lumber just received and for sale on the most reasonable terms: and all kinds of sawed materials of every description, suitable for housebuilding or water craft.

The demand for lumber in all dimensions was great. Such advertisements as the following which appeared in the *Herald* on September 23, 1830, are typical:

Cash. Noble and Hills will pay cash for the following materials if delivered soon. 14000 inch boards; 3000, 10 ft. long joists; Scantling, Siding 6000 ft. 2 inch planc, 4000 ft. hewn Oak timber and 90 Perch of Stone.

In addition to the imports from Canada, the volume demanded by the building operations of these years called for a large number of sawmills. The first was built by Kingsbury in 1800 on Mill Creek. It has been stated that Philo Scovill built another on Big Creek and entered the contracting business at an unspecified date, probably around 1816. There were certainly a large number of others in the immediate vicinity of Cleveland by 1830, inasmuch as the *Herald* stated there were 48 in Cuyahoga County in that year. Then, on April 7, 1831, this editorial was printed in the *Cleveland Herald*:

We have been requested to notify the citizens of a meeting at the house of Philo Scovill, on Saturday, April 9, to take measures for the erection of a steam sawmill in this village. The prospective growth of this village and consequent requisition for sawed Lumber, together with the frequent dearth of this kind of building material, inspires a belief that the proposed undertaking will be not only an incalculable benefit to the community, but a source of profit to the stockholders.

Such a statement reflects the demand for sawed lumber in the late 1820's.

Throughout this pre-canal era, wood remained the principal building material, but during these same years the builders began to exploit other materials as well. The shales in the vicinity of Cleveland were from fifty to one hundred feet thick and red burning, and were an ideal material for building brick. No record is available of the establishment of the first brick kiln, but 1814 is the date assigned to the first fabrication of this material. In that year J. A. and Irad Kelly built a brick store on Superior Street, and in the same year Alfred Kelley started his residence of the same material on Lake Street. Many others of brick construction followed, and in 1828, the second Court House was built of brick with stone and wood trim. As a more monumental and fireproof material, brick became increasingly popular as the decades passed.

Cut stone was the last material to be exploited for building purposes, despite its prevalence in the neighborhood. Outcrops of a fine grade of blue-gray Berea sandstone which weathered to a light buff were present in Cuyahoga County and later became very popular. These were exploited slowly at first, largely because of the comparative difficulty of working the material without power tools. Up to the time of the second Court House, on which stone trim was used, there is no evidence of any extensive use of stone in the buildings of Cleveland.

It is probable that a majority of the smaller buildings, private houses and stores, were built by amateur carpenters. Certainly there was no difficulty entailed in the construction of log houses which continued to be built in the 1820's and the framing of a small building required only a rudimentary knowledge of tools. But for the more elaborate structures including pretentious houses and public buildings, a higher degree of professional skill was demanded. No accurate count of the number of trained carpenters is available for these years, but a few names appear in the records.[37] Levi Johnson, the pioneer craftsman who produced the unique first Court House, was practising both as a carpenter and as a shipbuilder throughout this period. Philo Scovill was a trained carpenter and contractor and climaxed a long and successful practice in building by the construction in 1825 of his Franklin House and its later rebuilding and enlargement in 1845. The names of Henry L. Noble as designer and both Noble and George C. Hill as builders are connected with this Second Court House erected in 1826-1828 on the Public Square. Undoubtedly many more made their living by the practice of the building trades, though their names are not found before 1830.

None of these, of course, had formal architectural training. Levi Johnson and Philo Scovill were carpenters, builders, and contractors, and while certainly competent at their trades, they as certainly were artisans rather than professional designers. Henry L. Noble who is credited as the "designer" of the most pretentious building of the period, the second Court House, is listed in the directory of 1837 as "joiner and builder."

In these circumstances it is not surprising that few of the buildings of the period were of any architectural pretension. With wood as the principal building material and with a majority of the buildings erected by artisans, this was to be expected. But the small number of trained craftsman and the limitations placed upon their construction techniques were not the only explanations for the primitive character of the buildings before 1830. Cleveland during these fifteen years was just emerging from the frontier stage. Conditions had improved and amenities had been introduced since 1815, but the fact remains that the next decade and a half was in most respects an extension of the pioneer period. Ground-clearing was still a major problem. The rapid increase in population and the demand for numerous houses almost precluded fine style. Harvey Rice states that the majority of houses were small in 1824. Moreover, Cleveland remained during these decades a poor community. There is no indication of considerable wealth before the stimulation of the canals reached the port on the lake. No landed proprietors and no men of established fortunes came to the frontier. Even had the designers been available to create an architecture of dignity, the money to erect such buildings was not forthcoming.

In the absence of any pictorial record, one may visualize the town in 1830 as a mixture of log cabins remaining from the earlier period, as well as recently built, and small frame houses of few rooms and plain design. There were, however, a handful of more ambitious buildings, and it is on the basis of these that the architectural attainments of the community must be judged. Those for which there are sufficient records include the home of Alfred Kelley, the Academy, Trinity Church, several hotels, and finally the second Court House. Except for the Kelley house all of these date from the 1820's.

By that date Cleveland was no longer a frontier outpost. Immigration on an increasing scale and the improved means of intercourse with the east measurably reduced its provincial and pioneer character. This is quite evident in these first important buildings of the town. They are of a piece with the new spirit in architectural design which was emerging along the eastern seaboard. While the plan of Cleveland had been a traditional New England scheme, by the time these first significant buildings were erected a profound change had begun to take place in the architecture of the country. The traditional Georgian style was virtually at an end, even though it had by no means entirely disappeared. Its elegant proportions, its refinement and gentility had answered the needs of the eastern seaboard for almost a century, but it had too many associations with the English masters for the taste of the young Republic. After the Revolution the progressive architects in the east sought a style without the connotations of colonialism, and that search produced a new and dynamic phase in American art. Cleveland architecture was born in a period of ferment which marks the formation of the first consciously native style to emerge in the country.

The architectural forms which began to appear at the end of the century reflected the new spirit of the times. The American nation had just succeeded, after a bitter struggle, in breaking the ties with England and it demanded an architecture befitting this independence. The Colonial styles were no longer appropriate. A new form endowed with scale and dignity and with democratic associations was needed. Such an architecture began to appear in the last decade of the century and came to be known as the Federal Style. It was the product of many architects and appeared in several of the leading centers on the eastern seaboard at

virtually the same time. It was therefore, not so much a unified style as it was a ganglia of forms dedicated to the common aspiration of developing an architecture appropriate to the American democracy.

Leadership was provided by Thomas Jefferson. More than any single figure, Jefferson was responsible for the direction which architecture was to take in the decades 1790 to 1820. He detested the Baroque decadence of the English tradition and turned to the severity of the purer Palladianism and to the scale and boldness of Roman Art as correctives. Tentatively in the design of the Virginia State Capitol of 1789, more boldly and completely in the remodelling of Monticello between 1796 and 1809, and in a grand and formal arrangement in the University of Virginia in 1817 to 1825, Jefferson imbued his architecture with the simple and spacious forms he considered so vital to the times. This was no archaeological art, though its inspiration and many of its details were Roman, but a new and energetic architecture conceived for the service of the independent American nation. Its influence was enormous. Through the personal friendship and inspiration of Jefferson, the architecture of Thornton, Latrobe and Mills extended these ideals and placed upon the capital city of Washington the stamp of a distinct style.

The original Roman inspiration in the art of Jefferson was replaced in that of Latrobe and Mills by an addiction for Greek detail. The change was slight and did not diminish the clarity of design and the structural breadth which were the essential ingredients in this movement. The Bank of Pennsylvania by Latrobe in 1798 used Greek columns on a simple massive building surmounted by a dome of Roman profile. In the many government buildings by Mills, particularly in his Treasury Building, the monumental portico was Greek, but the structure of the building was massive and its ceilings vaulted. The National Capitol emerged, under the hands of a sequence of designers, as a monumental and impressive structure which was intended to be an appropriate symbol of the central government.

The center of this vital movement was Washington, D. C., but the same ideals infected other parts of the country as well. Latrobe and Mills carried their principles to Baltimore and Philadelphia and Strickland, a pupil of Latrobe, worked in Philadelphia and various parts of the south. In New York, the later work of McComb developed a massive and solid character despite its English and Continental leanings. In New England, with its cultural center at Boston, the ties with England were still strong and the traditional forms died more slowly. The early work of Charles Bulfinch likewise rests upon a knowledge of contemporary English practice acquired both through architectural books and by direct contact during his European travels. But in his late work there is a new sense of scale and a simpler treatment of surfaces. In such buildings as the Old City Hall in Boston in 1810 and in University Hall at Cambridge in 1813-15 he used a severe masonry and basic architectural form which conforms to the progressive ideals of the period. Due largely to his influence the subsequent Boston school under Asher Benjamin, Isaiah Rogers and Peter Banner created a simple and dignified style which reached fruition in the Greek Revival.

These were the major currents of progressive architectural taste in the decades on either side of 1800 in the east. One minor current, destined for a greater role to come also is to be found at this time. The Gothic Revival became a consistent movement only at a later date, but sporadic experiments with pseudo-Gothic details were common in this country before the end of the century. The first Trinity Church in New York, built in 1737, was a conventional meeting house except that it was trimmed with Gothic detail, and the second church which replaced this one in 1788-90 was in a simi-

lar hybrid style. After 1800 the number of these experiments with medieval forms increased. In 1805 Latrobe drew up an alternative Gothic design for the Baltimore Cathedral which was, however, rejected in favor of the classic building which still stands. A few years later in 1809, Bulfinch also tried his hand at Gothic design in the Federal Street Church in Boston. This was once again a conventional meeting house to which a few rather irrelevant-looking Gothic details on cupola and interior were added. While it is quite clear that none of these designers had any real understanding of the style with which they were attempting to deal, in the next decades such architects as A. J. Davis and Richard Upjohn produced more knowledgeable buildings which were the precursors of a widespread Gothic Revival.

At the same time architectural training was undergoing an important change. After 1800 formal professional education became a factor in American architecture. Jefferson, Thornton and Bulfinch were at best semi-professional designers, each with a library of volumes on the subject and each partially trained in the practice of the art. On the other hand, Benjamin Latrobe came to this country with a complete professional training and Robert Mills claimed with some justice to be the first native American to receive a thorough architectural education. Now too the first architectural publications by American designers spread this professional knowledge widely over the eastern states. Starting with the books of Asher Benjamin, followed by those of Minard Lafever and others, publications which were consciously American became available to the carpenter and builder, and disseminated the new taste across the country.

These new forms were gradually to change the course of American design and to culminate in the Greek Revival within the next decades. They were brought into being by the leading architects in the cultural centers along the eastern seaboard, in Washington, Philadelphia, New York and Boston especially. But the long tradition of the Georgian style did not die in a decade. In the small towns and in the countryside change took place more slowly. The artisan tended to use the forms to which he and his clients were inured, and most rural and small town architecture remained essentially Georgian until the full establishment of the Greek Revival in the late 1830's and 1840's.

The situation in the east when Cleveland was starting its architectural career was, then, a fluid one dominated by a vigorous new spirit with a will to create a native American style. Old-fashioned Georgian forms remained along with an Americanized English tendency in the late Colonial, and a few experimental Gothic details. The advanced designers were, however, creating a harmonious style, particularly in public buildings, which had new scale and monumentality and on which an indigenous architecture could be built. These contemporary movements were soon reflected in the buildings of Cleveland.

Chronologically the earliest important building in Cleveland was the residence of Alfred Kelley, which was completed probably during the year 1817 (Figure 7). It was reputedly the first residence of brick to be built in the village. No descriptions of any value exist, but a drawing gives a quite adequate idea of its appearance. It was a solidly built house, consisting of a cubical central pavilion covered by a gable roof flanked by smaller wings. In the facade of the main section the doorway and two oblong windows were set each in its own arched recess and an oval light was let into the pediment of the main gable. The doors and windows were unframed except for a stone sill and lintel and the only moldings were simple projections of the brick courses. For all this, the house had the good proportions of a professional design. In the midst of the log cabins and frame houses of the village this residence was referred to with pride and it was, in fact, a quite impressive house to appear as early as 1817 in the village of Cleveland, perhaps the first indication of the emergence of the town from its status as a frontier community. The use of the enclosing arches and the simple wall treatment with openings are

characteristics to be found in Benjamin's architectural manuals. Such plans are also found in Benjamin and were becoming prevalent in the east, especially in New York State. In general terms this house had the character of the "late Colonial" style and the simplicity of form which reflect the new ideals being developed in the east.

The second building of interest to be erected in Cleveland was the Academy (Figure 8). This replaced the small log structure which had been built in 1817 as the first formal school in the village. By 1821 this had been outgrown and a more commodious school house was needed. On June 6, 1822, the *Cleaveland Leader* announced:

> A neat and convenient Academy, built of brick, with a handsome spire, and with a spacious room in the second story, designed for public uses, is now nearly completed.

Andrew Freese gives this additional information about the building in his history of the early schools of the city: it was located opposite the first school on St. Clair Street, measured 45 by 25 feet and was of two floors. The lower floor was divided into two rooms, which were used for school purposes; the single upper chamber was at first rented out to churches and other organizations for assembly purposes; within a few years the upper floor was also required as a school room.

The drawing of the Academy indicates that it was a severely plain building. It rested on a low basement of stone, and stone slabs capped the end walls and chimney. The main body of the building was, however, of brick, while the pediment, window frames and octagonal spire were of wood. It was a simple oblong in plan except for the projecting stair tower on one side. The end walls, in which double chimneys were imbedded, rose above the gable roof with one deep setback to the chimneys. These forms were traditional ones which had been in use in the east, in both public and private buildings, for over a century. The shape

Figure 7. Alfred Kelley House, 1814-1817.

Figure 8. The Academy, 1821-1822.

Figure 9.
First Franklin House,
1826.

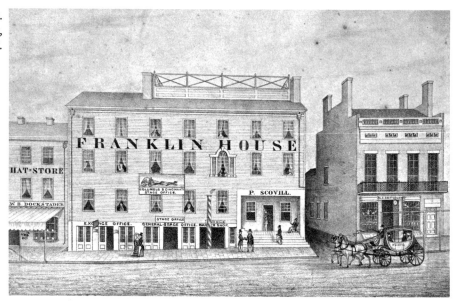

of the end walls, the gable and cupola, all stem from Georgian practice. This is, however, a very simplified version of the elegant eastern tradition and the reason for its rudimentary character is not far to seek. It was erected at public expense, at a time when the town was far from thriving and its severely simple forms were dictated largely by economy. Moreover there were in Cleveland at this time few highly-skilled artisans capable of the sophisticated craftsmanship of the full Georgian style.

In any case the Academy is an example of the extension to the midwest of an already old-fashioned tradition adapted in its simplest terms to the needs and abilities of the small community. It served its purpose for many years and was finally torn down in 1850 when more modern and spacious school buildings were needed.

Several hotels were erected in the period, of which the first Franklin House, built by Philo Scovill was the most ambitious (Figure 9). The owner inserted this advertisement in the *Cleaveland Herald* on July 21, 1826:

> Franklin House, Cleaveland, Ohio. The subscriber informs the public that he has just completed a large and convenient House, situated on the North side of Superior Street, between Bank and Water Streets. It is three stories high, very spacious, furnished in a style not surpassed in this part of the state, and is now open for reception of Guests .... P. Scovill, Cleaveland, July 21, 1826.

Like its predecessors this was a frame structure but, as advertised, was the largest hotel to date in the town. No detailed information on its internal arrangements is available, but the appearance of the facade has been preserved in a print. The three floors arose above a low basement given over to shops except in the right-hand corner where steps to the hotel entrance were located. The walls were severely plain and the eaves line simple, but there were two features of interest in this design. Two thirds of the roof is surmounted, between chimneys, by a flimsy imitation of the Georgian "widow's walk" and the row of plain double-

hung sash windows at the second floor level is broken by a Palladian window just above and to the left of the entrance door. In an otherwise simple building these two Georgian details seem to reflect that nostalgia for New England which characterized the village as a whole.

The most important building of the period, was the second Court House, built in 1828. The old Court House in 1812 by Levi Johnson had served for many years while the population of Cleveland was rapidly growing and by 1826 the county commissioners decided a more spacious and modern structure was needed. The first notice to appear in the newspapers of their intentions was published on June 9, 1826, which called for bids for brick, and in a second notice a few months later for the stone and wood required. In March of 1827, the firm of Henry L. Noble and George C. Hill was commissioned to construct the building and it was completed by October, 1828. An interesting sidelight on the building methods at that time is offered by I. A. Morgan:[38]

> I helped build the second court house, which was a brick structure, and for that reason it was supposed it would outlast a century. It occupied the ground where the south corner fountain now is, as many who saw it before it was taken down remember. All the doors and sash for it were made by hand, and the flooring dressed by hand. There was no labor-saving machinery to do a part of the work of carpenters when the second court house was constructed.

This building, the most ambitious project to date in Cleveland, was then a brick building with wooden floors and trim and with some stone used in its construction. Its specifications were laid down by the County Commissioners, and it was built by a firm of contractors and builders. The work of shaping its materials was a matter of hand labor, even to the details of sash, door-frames and floor finishing. Such conditions are one explanation for the relative simplicity of the average building at this date.

Figure 10. Public Square in 1839.

The most complete description of the Court House is given in the *Directory* of 1837:[39]

> It is a brick building, two stories high; the front is ornamented with stone antaes or pilasters of the Dorick [sic] order, supporting a Dorick entablature; the whole is crowned by an Ionic belfry and dome. On the ground floor are the departments for county officers. The court room is on the second floor.

It appears in a painting of the Public Square attributed to Sebastian Heine and dated 1839, which now hangs in the Western Reserve Historical Society (Figure 10). In this picture the Court House dominates the Public Square, on the borders of which the small frame houses are in marked contrast to the scale of the new building. It is a square block of a building raised on a low stone basement with an entablature which encompasses all sides of the structure, also of stone, which is carved into a rather crude interpretation of the architrave of a Doric order. The principal facade facing north on the Square is ornamented by six pilasters, four of which support a flattened pediment into which a depressed semicircular fan light has been let. It has a flattened hipped roof with two balustrades, one at the eaves and a second at the base of the central cupola above.

The first impression given by this building is that it is a conservative design (Figure 11). The low relief of the mouldings and pilasters, the use of balustrades and fan-light in the pediment suggest the traditional English forms. The scheme as a whole was a common one, to be found frequently in the east. But the Adam detail of the older style, the windows recessed under arches and the small scale of columns, entablatures and balustrades, are now gone. This is, in fact, a Federal Style building. It has the severity and simple block form of the new manner and in particular the full entablature and large scale order of a classical style. In these respects, the second Court House was the only build-

ing in Cleveland before 1830 to incorporate the progressive spirit which dominated the architecture of the east during the preceding decades. Considering the conditions of hand craftsmanship, economic limitations, and the fact that Cleveland was just emerging from the pioneer state, this building was an attainment of considerable significance and reflects the national artistic revolution of these years.

The first church building to be erected in Cleveland dates from the following year. In contrast to the Federal Style dignity of the Court House, the almost contemporary Trinity Church was a flimsy frame structure of that same misunderstood Gothic which was found in the east in the previous decades (Figure 12). It was first noticed in the newspapers in May of 1828 in an advertisement calling for materials to be used in its construction, and was completed by July of 1829. On August 12, 1829, the church formally commenced its career. George Merwin is a firsthand authority for its location:[40]

> The first church, built in 1828, was Trinity Church on the southeast corner of Seneca and St. Clair, a commodious frame building that was destroyed by fire about the year 1853 [sic].

The Trinity Cathedral *Guide* provides this interesting item regarding the history of this building:[41]

> In 1833 . . . the church was enlarged by the singular method of cutting the building in two and placing a new piece sixteen and a half feet long, in the center.

In 1837 the town's first *Directory* gives a brief description:[42]

> It is a handsome frame building, constructed in the Gothic order, measures 70 x 40 feet, and is finished with a bell section and four Gothic points or spires.

The Trinity Cathedral *Guide* adds that "The exterior of the church was painted white, relieved by green blinds."

The church appears several times in Whelpley views of

Figure 11. Second Court House, 1828.

Cleveland executed in 1833. He represents it as a frame edifice built on a low foundation of masonry or brick, oblong in plan and surmounted by a simple gable roof. There is a single entrance in the base of a square tower which projects half its depth from the center of the west facade. The doorway is deeply splayed and is flanked by high lancet windows and the side walls are penetrated by four more smaller lancets. All the openings are pointed. The first stage of the tower has a triple lancet, and all four faces of the upper stage again have pointed windows. The whole is surmounted by four steeply pointed spires. In the main body of the church the surface is of horizontally placed matched boards, while in the tower and pediment, the boards are placed vertically. The corners of the church and tower are reinforced by pilaster-like boards and horizontal boards run beneath the eaves and under the raking cornice. The splayed doorway has wooden imitations of archivolts.

Altogether a curious hybrid character was produced in this building. Its overall external arrangements were those of the traditional meeting house, but the flush matchedboards were an innovation of the classical revival. The proportions of the wide boards under the eaves and raking cornice also were more classical than Georgian. All the other details, however, were Gothic. The lancet windows, a pointed, deeply splayed doorway, and the crenellations and spires have the flimsy pseudo-Gothic character which had occasionally been seen in the east during the preceding decades.

Unfortunately very little idea regarding the interior dispositions of this interesting church can be obtained. No drawing nor photograph of it exists. A brief description by Henderson states merely that it had a "gallery over the entrance, and a projecting chancel, guarded by a semi-circular railing . . . , all bore witness to the simple and patriarchal tastes of the congregation"[43] (Figure 13).

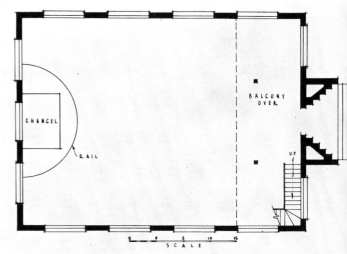

Figure 12. Trinity Church, 1828-1829.

Figure 13. Plan of Trinity Church, 1828-1829.

The congregation of Trinity began to overcrowd the old church in the 1840's, and several congregations were detached in the following decade. By 1853, despite these departures, the congregation was again overcrowding the ancient building, and a new structure was projected. Before it could be built Trinity Church burned on March 30, 1854.

This small handful of significant buildings provides clues to the character of the town's culture in these early years. They were built during the decades which saw an important revolution in the course of eastern architectural development, but with the exception of the Court House the Cleveland buildings were scarcely effected. In 1817 the Kelley House was fairly up-to-date but in the next decade the traditional forms of the Franklin Hotel and the Academy and the thin character of the Gothic detail of Trinity Church were already outmoded. As in the plan of the town, so in its architecture, the frontier village was dominated by conservatism.

During the transition from a primitive frontier community to a developed village from 1815 to 1830, the character of the embryo city of Cleveland had been changed in many respects. To accommodate a seven-fold population increase the town had expanded rapidly first by subdivision of the northwest sector, and then by expansion to the south and later eastward. Most of this development followed established eastern precedents, but at the end of the period the important innovation of a diagonal street was introduced, forecasting a new era in city design for Cleveland which was to be developed further in the period of the canals. Meantime a relaxation of the extreme demands of pioneer life permitted the introduction of many amenities. In addition to new opportunities on intellectual lines including newspapers, a forum and bookstore, schools and church organizations, the town began to acquire, in a limited number of instances, a more sophisticated architectural quality. These buildings reflected the heterogeneous character of the previous decades in the east, rather than the controlling harmony of the new spirit which was growing in the cultural centers.

A new era was making itself felt in Cleveland by 1830. The completion of the canal in 1827, once the cumulative effect of its stimulation was felt, created many changes in the fortunes of the town and as significant changes, for better and also for worse, in its appearance and its solution of physical problems.

CHAPTER THREE

THE MERCANTILE TOWN 1830-1854

Between 1830, when the stimulation of the canals began to be felt in the port city of Cleveland, and 1854, when it was united with its smaller western neighbor, Ohio City, to become a single metropolis, extensive changes occurred in the appearance and character of the town. As transportation from the East improved and fares were reduced, the population grew, and to accommodate the increase the town limits had several times to be extended and new streets laid out. The established businesses prospered and new ones appeared in large numbers to produce a thriving mercantile center. But with prosperity there arrived also the harassing problems of a municipality. During the brief period of little more than two decades the town passed from the simple existence of a village to the complexities of city life, and the very speed of the transformation in itself magnified the difficulties involved. Whole areas of the city changed rapidly; the problems of paving and lighting streets and of providing an adequate water supply arose. Sanitation and recreation facilities became imperative. Real estate speculation accompanied the pressures of population increase, and a variety of architectural styles competed for latest honors. By mid-century Cleveland had arrived at the very brink of the complexity which has come to characterize the modern city. The adaptations successfully made and the failures suffered during this evolution are characteristic of the

period. This is the soil in which the contemporary city has its roots.

This quarter century is, in fact, the crucial one in the development of Cleveland. During these decades of mercantile expansion the present characteristics of the center of the city were established. To a high degree the arrangements then made and the precedents then laid down are those with which the present city has had to abide.

The 1830's and 1840's were the canal period in the history of Cleveland and of Ohio. Until the advent of the railroads at mid-century, no single influence had a more stimulating effect upon the state and specifically upon those towns located along the waterways. Many towns benefited but none more so than those which were situated, like Cleveland, at terminal points of the canals. The wisdom of Cleveland's founders in choosing a site with the potentialities of an important port was substantiated during these decades.

As early as 1817 when work on the Erie Canal in New York State was begun, agitation commenced for a comparable project in Ohio.[44] Investigation committees were appointed, commissioners assigned to locate possible routes and several surveys made, but it was not until 1825 that work was actually under way. Fortunately for Cleveland the route determined upon led from Lake Erie up the Cuyahoga Valley to the old Portage Path and thence by devious channels to the Ohio. The first segment was that joining Cleveland and Akron, which was completed by 1827, and five years later the lake was finally linked by water to the Ohio River. In subsequent years branch lines were established in various parts of the state until the network connected a large number of the interior counties to the water highways of the lake and river to the north and south. These were destined to carry a large proportion of the interior commerce of the state until after mid-century when railroad transportation became a serious rival which ultimately destroyed the prosperity of the canals.

Meantime the state had immeasurably benefited. For the first time the products of the farm country of the interior were given easy access to markets. Prices of local goods rose, while those of imports fell as transportation costs from the east were reduced. The volume of traffic at Cleveland is clearly indicated by the tolls collected. In 1836, $60,583.36 were paid, and this figure rose steadily to a high of $90,-874.20 in 1850. Thereafter the competition of the railroads increased yearly, and the canals declined until at Cleveland the infinitesimal toll of $21.45 was collected in 1907. Passenger traffic was even more adversely affected. In 1839, 19,962 passengers arrived at Cleveland via canal. This figure was approximately maintained until 1842 but thereafter declined rapidly. In 1851, after the railroad had entered Cleveland, only 5,387 arrivals are recorded and by 1855 not a single passenger entered the town on the canalboats.[45]

The volume of shipping on the lake rose simultaneously.[46] Sailing vessels were built in mounting numbers during those years. By 1841, some 250 such vessels were in operation on the lake. These were mostly small ships of from 50 to 100 tons with an occasional vessel up to 350 tons, but the volume of freight transported rose steadily. In 1831, 355 sailing vessels reached the port. Thirteen years later in 1844, this number had increased to 1,561.

After mid-century the steam-propelled vessel gradually replaced the sailing ship on the lake. The first steam craft

were side-wheelers. Ever since the famous Walk-in-the-Water of 1818 both the number and size of these ships steadily increased, particularly after 1831. In 1839, over thirty were in operation and by 1850 the side-wheel steamer was at the height of its popularity, reaching sizes up to 2,000 tons. It was used largely for passenger traffic, however, and was seriously affected by the advent of the railroad. Water travel was too slow and in the late 1850's these picturesque ships practically disappeared from the lakes. Propeller-driven ships replaced them starting with the Vandalia which reached Lake Erie via the Welland Canal in 1842. These were better suited to freight transport and were more easily accommodated to the canals. Hence they have continued to the present day to compete successfully with the railroads in the handling of heavy bulk loads.

Sporadic harbor improvements kept pace with the increased tonnage to reach Cleveland. The channel attained a depth of eleven feet by 1833 and repairs on the piers were undertaken in the 1840's. Meantime silting of the inner harbor necessitated constant dredging. Despite Federal appropriations, much of the burden of upkeep and improvement by means of piers and levees had to be supported by private funds, and a continual struggle was under way throughout this period to accommodate the expanding harbor traffic.

Highway transportation also developed rapidly during these decades. The character of the North, Central and South Highways as public roads was assured by enactment of a law to that effect by the legislature on February 11, 1832. Even earlier, in 1830, the ancient path to Tinkers Creek was made a state road which followed the present route of Broadway to Newburg. This was named Pittsburg Street. The route through Solon and Auburn to Pittsburgh was surveyed by Ahaz Merchant in 1833 and became a state road, and the road from the east to Chardon was extended into Cleveland as a state highway in the same year. Another important route which was improved in these years led from Brooklyn through Strongsville and southward. By these various routes Cleveland was more adequately connected to east and south and overland transport was greatly encouraged. Despite state support, which was abandoned after the opening of the canals, the condition of these roads was, in the main, intolerable and private corporations took over their layout and maintenance. Charging toll fees as compensation for the expense entailed, these companies managed to make the roads passable in all weather. Planking became standard practice in the 1840's and was steadily extended in the next decade.

The improvement and increasing number of roads, in turn, encouraged stage lines. Competition became rife in the 1830's with a large number of stages operating to the south and east and at least one to Toledo and Detroit. Passenger traffic increased accordingly while the Conestoga wagons, capable of handling from five to ten tons of goods, were used to transport freight of light weight and sufficient value to pay for the relatively high cost of this service.

By all these means the population was augmented and served, and the expanding economy of Cleveland stimulated. The population of Cleveland, which was 1,075 in 1830, climbed to 6,071 in a decade and reached 17,034 by mid-century. Every stage, every canalboat and ship which entered port added to the population of the thriving community. In 1853 the city directory referred proudly to a population of "30,000 souls."[48]

All of these changes, the improved communication systems by land and water, the mounting prosperity, and the prodigious increase in population, were but local indices to the growth and development of the midwest. In this period the region west of the Appalachians was losing its frontier status. With a rapidity which could never have been anticipated the western lands were cleared for cultivation, roads

and canals developed which opened all parts of the region, and towns and cities founded. Long before the Civil War the west had become an integral part of the national scene and the western cities were capable of making their own contribution to American culture.

To meet the demands of the enormous increase in population in this twenty-four year period the lateral expansion of the city was accelerated. The modest addition made in 1829 was merely the first of a series which extended the official town limits before the union of Cleveland and Ohio City in 1854. In 1834 an act of the General Assembly annexed the flat land within the first big bend in the river, an area soon to be known as "Cleveland Centre." The same act added a large area to the east and south of the village limits, pushing the boundary east to Perry Street (East 22nd) and south to include the two-acre lots south of Ohio Street together with the area between Broadway and the river to the west (C, Figure 6). When the village was incorporated as the City of Cleveland in 1836, a large addition was made which lay roughly west of Perry Street and north of the line of ten-acre lots on the south (D, Figure 6). These outlines served the city for 14 years, but in 1850 the largest addition yet to be made was the annexation of the ten-acre lots (E, Figure 6).

The period was climaxed by the union of Cleveland with the smaller town of Ohio City west of the river in 1854.

Many new streets were laid out in these additions and in the older quarter as well. Since the immediate effect of the opening of the canal was to stimulate commercial activity, the first new streets added after 1830 were adjacent to the port itself. In 1833, four were laid out to subdivide the area between Water Street and the river. River Street (West 11th) was opened along the bank of the Cuyahoga, Spring Street (West 10th) was surveyed parallel to Water between it and the river with Lighthouse Street at right angles to it, and a diagonal street on the side hill, Meadow, (West 11th Place) led from Lighthouse to Bath. These supplied the frontages and the traffic lanes demanded by the business brought by the canals and lake traffic, and provided locations near the port for several small industries. In the next year, increased overland travel was reflected in the widening of Pittsburgh Street which was rapidly becoming the through way to the south via Newburgh. In 1835 the number of streets surveyed and opened is too numerous for complete listing. The population had risen suddenly to over 5,000 people and the town limits had again been enlarged the year before. Expansion was rapid and the new streets blossomed on all sides. Fortunately, in October of this year an accurate map was published by the county surveyor Ahaz Merchant (Figure 14).

This map shows a number of interesting developments in the plan of Cleveland. Within the area of the original town, guidance of the city council seems to have controlled the street pattern. The four new streets of 1833 already noted are recorded on this map. Several alleys and new streets —*i.e.,* York (Hamilton), Walnut and Chestnut (Chester) —subdivided the blocks north and east of the Square on the accepted oblong plan; so also Bolivar and Eagle, south of Huron. The precedent of Prospect Street, diagonal to the checkboard, now began to bear fruit. Lake and Prospect were extended and South Highway was brought in to the end of Ontario in addition to the widening of Pittsburgh. Thus two radiating streets were extended and two additional radiating streets were added before 1835, to provide more ready communication to south and east from the center of town.

These new radiating avenues were connected by a growing number of cross streets which followed the lines of division between the "out-lots" as surveyed back in 1797. It is of interest to note that the original design of these lots thus controlled the expansion of the town for many decades.

So far the expansion of the town was undertaken in orderly fashion and appears to have been directed by the council. But at this same period there began a less salutary influence. Between 1833 and 1836 several important allotments were made on the outskirts and these were real estate speculations for personal profit. The earliest of these was the most interesting as a design. In 1833 Richard Hilliard, Edmund Clark and James S. Clark laid out and offered for sale all the land enclosed by the first big bend in the river, an area which was beyond the city limits at the time and hence outside the jurisdiction of the council. They laid out a straight road from near the canal basin, across the loop of land and over the bridge spanning the river which they had built for this purpose. This was labeled Columbus Street, and the bridge was, of course, Columbus Street Bridge. Bisecting this street a hub appropriately named Gravity Place was established and a series of radiating streets was laid out extending to the periphery of the plot. Intersecting these streets in a manner to form two sides of three squares, six additional streets were designed. The result bears a striking resemblance to the system of streets radiating from traffic circles and superimposed upon a gridiron which was established for Washington D. C., by Major L'Enfant many years before. So systematic an application of this characteristic Baroque scheme had not appeared prior to this time in the vicinity.

Although it was apparently the intention of this group of speculators to attract residences to this area, the depression of 1837 destroyed their schemes. The lots were sold by the sheriff and when business confidence was restored they were taken up for mercantile and industrial purposes.

The other large allotments were far less original in conception but left more serious scars upon the pattern of Cleveland. Two of them were subdivisions of town lots, and the third lay in the ten-acre lots. All entailed the laying out of a multiplicity of streets and alleys which were narrow and closely spaced, a sure indication of land speculation. These three areas may be seen on Merchant's map of 1835.

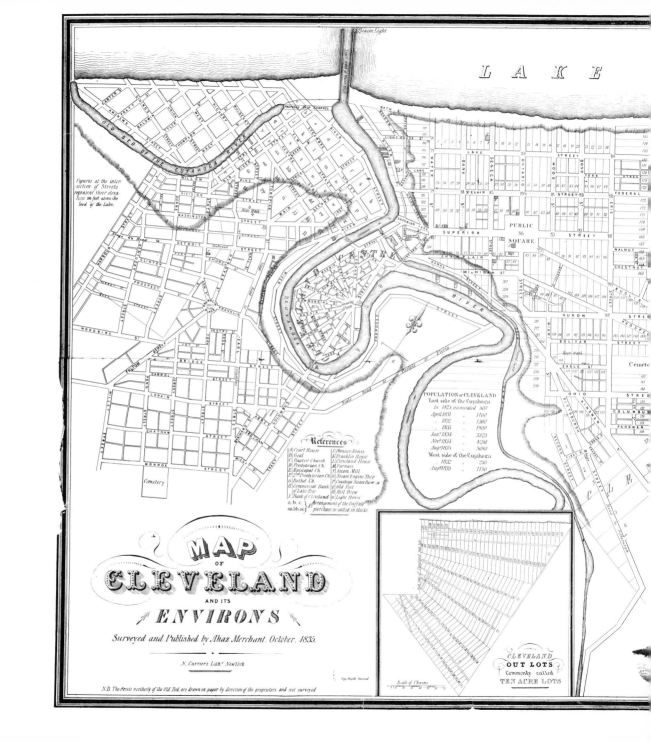

L A K E

Beacon Light

Figures at the inter-
section of Streets
represent their eleva-
tion in feet above the
level of the Lake.

References

A. Court House	J. Mansion House
B. Goal	K. Franklin House
C. Baptist Church	L. Cleveland House
D. Presbyterian Ch.	M. Furnace
E. Episcopal Ch.	N. Steam Mill
F. 2d Presbyterian Ch.	O. Steam Engine Shop
G. Bethel Ch.	P. Cuyahoga Steam Furnace
H. Commercial Bank	Q. Old Fort
of Lake Erie	R. Hill Brow
I. Bank of Cleveland	S. Light House
a. b. c. &c.	Arrangement of the Buffalo
aa. bb. cc.	purchase so called in blocks

POPULATION OF CLEVELAND
East side of the Cuyahoga

In 1825, numerated	500
April 1831	1100
1832	1300
1833	1900
Jan.y 1834	3323
Nov.r 1834	4250
Aug.st 1835	5080

West side of the Cuyahoga

| 1832 | 250 |
| Aug.st 1835 | 1150 |

MAP
OF
CLEVELAND
AND ITS
ENVIRONS

Surveyed and Published by Ahaz Merchant, October, 1835.

N. Currier's Lith.y New York

N.B. The Streets northerly of the Old Bed, are drawn on paper by direction of the proprietors and not surveyed

Scale of Chains

CLEVELAND
OUT LOTS
Commonly called
TEN ACRE LOTS

Copy Right Secured

The lines of the inn and out Lots as originally located are entered and their numbers are expressed within their respective lines in figures. Each inn Lot has 132 feet front and Each out Lot 330 feet front.

E R I E

WILSON STREET

Clinton Square

WILYON STREET

AIR ROAD

STREET

The following shows the number of vessels entered and cleared at the port of Cleveland with cargoes, and their aggregate tonnage from AD 1825 to August 10 1835.

Years	No. of vessels arrived with cargoes	No. of vessels cleared with cargoes	Aggregate tonnage of vessels arrival with cargoes	Aggregate tonnage of vessels cleared with cargoes	No. of vessels arrived from foreign ports	No. of vessels cleared for foreign ports	No. of Steam Boat arrival	No. of Steam Boats cleared	Total No. of arrivals including Steam Boats	Total amt of tonnage arrived including Steam Boats
1825	54	54	2060	2060	1	1	21	21	75	7380
1826	63	63	2855	2835	4	4	42	42	105	13135
1827	75	75	3000	3000	11	11	63	63	138	18750
1828	92	92	4440	4440	4	4	70	70	162	21640
1829	222	222	8840	8880	7	7	90	90	314	31300
1830	327	327	15449	15449	2	2	448	448	775	127449
1831	424	424	31407	31407	9	9	450	450	874	145907
1832	600	600	45082	45082	34	34	470	470	1070	182582
1833	800	800	56250	56250	125	125	705	705	1505	232500
1834	875	890	70000	71300	70	75	970	970	1845	341000
1835	437	445	43700	44600	67	81	454	435	892	113996

Street Road to Bufalo

In the first the two-acre lots between Lake and St. Clair just to the east of Erie Street were surveyed into allotments and sold by a group of speculators headed by Lee Canfield and Sheldon Pease. This was in 1835. In the same year the block south of the cemetery was likewise subdivided by Ashbel Walworth and Thomas Kelley.[49] In both allotments the tracts were subdivided by streets and narrow alleys which reduced the building sites to shallow lots. Thus the operators were assured of a handsome profit through the soaring land values of this period of expansion.

The third allotment was designed along quite other lines. Just beyond the city limits near the shore of the lake Canfield and Pease located Clinton Square in 1835 and sold the adjoining lots under elaborate provisions intended to insure the continued privacy of this area.[50] The owners of these lots around the square were to assume responsibility for its maintenance in return for its private use.

It is unfortunate that this experiment failed. Its intention was sound: to control a residential area in a manner to preserve its openness and livability, a sort of zoning operation which might have preserved the integrity of residential streets in the growing city. Though developed by speculators for personal profit, this scheme included a concept neglected by other allotments in the city, the guided development of a residential area. It was, however, never imitated in other parts of the city and it was borne down by the depression of 1837. The homes already there were either moved away or torn down and the location of the railroad nearby after 1851 ended once and for all this sole early experiment with residential community development.

In these five years of rapid expansion a pattern of development was established which controlled later street de-

Figure 14. Plan of Cleveland, 1835.

sign: the subdivision of the large blocks at the center was controlled to prevent overcrowding on narrow streets; the multiplication of radiating streets to south and east provided communication to the edge of town as wheeled traffic increased; the connecting streets between these radiating avenues permitted the necessary cross-traffic and at the same time preserved the real estate values by following lot lines; in most areas the individual plots were generous in size. At the same time real estate speculation, inevitable under an expanding economy, took some toll in the form of narrow sites and a multiplicity of streets. As early as 1835 both the best and the worst aspects of the design of the modern center of Cleveland had established their roots.

As the population swelled from 5,000 in 1835 to some 30,000 in 1853, the lateral expansion of the city was correspondingly accelerated. And it is notable that the precedents established by 1835 were followed in the expansion without significant change. At the end of the mercantile period in 1853 a quite accurate *Directory* map was issued which records the expansion since 1835 (Figure 15). Subdivision of the central area by parallel streets and extension of the outskirts by radiating avenues are the means employed in this expansion. There is also some evidence here of speculation under the pressures of rapid expansion, but in general the order imposed by the original pie-shaped segments designed in 1797 controlled the eastward development of the city in these decades.

Accompanying this rapid lateral expansion of the town, important changes were made in its character and appearance. Mere extension in itself transformed what had been a small village into a sprawling town. But the center became built up in some sectors to the point of overcrowding as well. The character of whole areas of town was modified as the process continued. The wholesale district expanded mightily. The residential district spread outward as the re-

tail concerns took over the central areas. New industries were developed and competed with the mercantile firms for space on the flats. New demands were met by new building types and new methods of construction. Altogether the period from 1830 to 1854 transfigured the entire face of the town.

It is possible to visualize these changes with some accuracy. After 1830 pictorial records are for the first time available in quantity. The appearance of the town at the beginning of the canal period is well recorded, thanks largely to Thomas Whelpley who made a number of prints of the village from as many station points in 1833.

One of his prints now in the Western Reserve Historical Society shows the Cuyahoga River valley as seen from the west side at that date (Figure 16). From this vantage point the town appears to be a small village with a scattering of houses on the plateau above the river. On the flats the new commercial activity had already resulted in numerous warehouses from the river mouth to Cleveland Centre. Six large ships, at least two of which are side-wheelers, are represented in the channel. Though the town above still gives the appearance of a small village, the source of its future prosperity is apparent in the activity along the river.

The character of the residential center of town is shown in a second print, a view toward the east on St. Clair Street near Bank in the same year (Figure 17). Some of the principal buildings in town are represented: the Academy, Trinity Church, the recently completed Presbyterian Church and at the extreme right, the second Court House. Scattered in between lie the small houses, each facing on the street, with generous yards enclosed by picket fences. The orderly arrangement of the large plots is obvious and gives to the town at this time the spacious regularity of a New England village.

Figure 15. Plan of Cleveland, 1853.

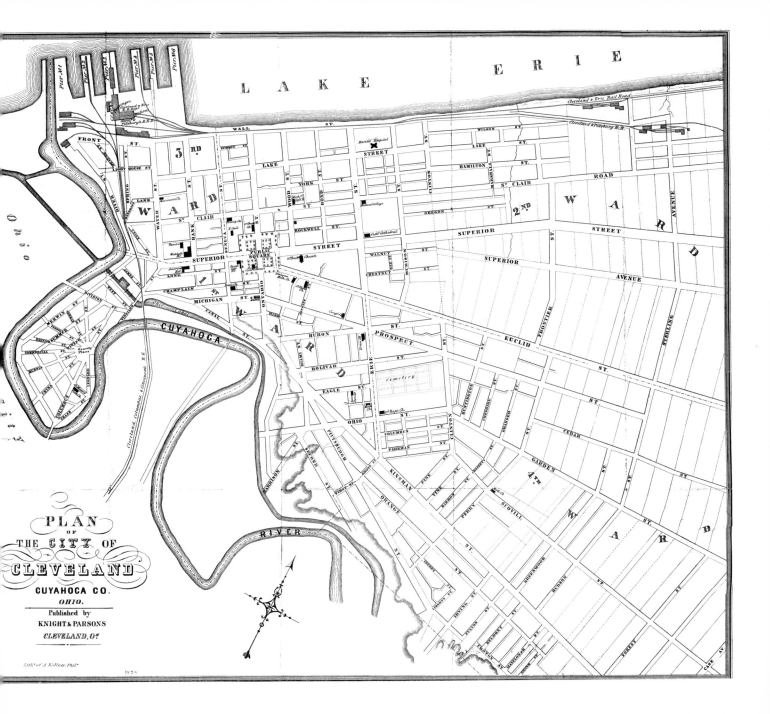

PLAN OF THE CITY OF CLEVELAND CUYAHOCA CO. OHIO. Published by KNIGHT & PARSONS CLEVELAND, O.

Figure 17. Cleveland, looking east from Bank and St. Clair in 1833.

Figure 16. Cleveland from Brooklyn Hill in 1833.

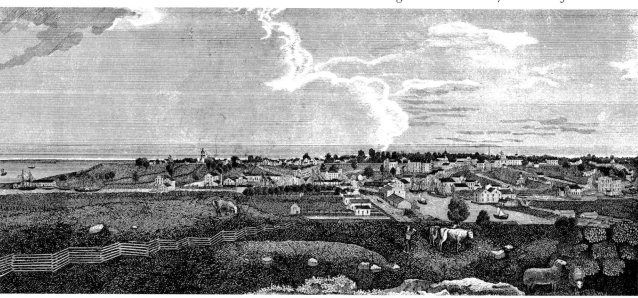

Figure 18. Public Square in 1833.

The same area appears again from the opposite view in the print of the Public Square, which shows also the Cleveland Hotel and the length of Superior Street (Figure 18). In 1833 this was the retail district, although private houses are still interspersed between the stores. Characteristically the buildings range side by side in close order in contrast to the spacious design of the residential area beyond, giving to the street its stamp of a commercial center. In view of the development of three and four story brick business blocks which was to take place in the next years, it may be noted that the stores which line Superior in 1833 still resemble private dwellings. They are mostly of wooden construction and are generally one story or two stories in height.

From these prints the impression is to be had of an open village with gathering wholesale and shipping business along its waterfront, and but a single retail business street and a residential area of small frame dwellings. Except for the absence of large shade trees the town by 1833 had taken on the character envisaged by its founders, that of a new England village. Had Cleveland, like so many other towns of the Western Reserve, remained a backwater in the coming phase of mercantile expansion, this ideal might well have been preserved. Its location at the mouth of the river precluded this possibility. Commercial expansion was foreordained by its site, and within a matter of years this idyllic character was lost. By the end of the canal period a new town had emerged, hardly recognizable as a descendant of the quiet village of 1833.

The growth of the town in the next decades under the impetus of the canals and lake traffic is indicated by newspaper comment. On October 13, 1831, the *Cleveland Herald* states optimistically:

> We have nine large warehouses and several others are being constructed. A steam flouring mill, an air furnace, and steam engine manufactory, a dry dock, a paper mill, twenty different kinds of stores, two printing offices, a brewery, and a pail factory soon to be erected. The various trades are pursued with profit, and journeymen have been in demand, particularly carpenters and joiners to which may be attributed the fact there is not even a room to be rented and families have been compelled to take shelter in barns.

And again in January of 1833 the *Herald* says:

> The business on the lake has increased one hundred percent since 1830. The great difficulty of procuring building materials has prevented the erection of buildings, but during the past year ninety-six buildings have been built. In this group there are two stone buildings, one a county jail and the other a Presbyterian Church . . . .

The dearth of buildings, particularly of dwellings, was to become a recurrent complaint in the next few years. In 1835 the population was around 5,000, an increase of more than two and one-half fold in five years. It is not surprising that the builders failed to keep pace and that an anonymous writer is quoted by the *Whig* in December of that year:

> There is an evil among us, which unless speedily removed, will direct the tide of emigration [sic] to some other commercial center, and give a blow to our prosperity, from which we may never recover. It is the want of comfortable and convenient dwelling houses.

Nor were accommodations for travellers in better case it seems. The *Herald* editorialized on the situation in June of the next year:

> What are our enterprising businessmen — men of capital about that they do not make better arrangements for the accommodation of the public, and for those who wish to take up their residence among us?

The influx of new residents was considerably slowed by the depression in the next years and the builders apparently had an opportunity to catch up with the demand, for the complaints cease in the 1840's. In the fifties, however, a new influx of prospective residents again caused a shortage. The *Daily True Democrat* on March 13, 1851, has this to say:

> The only drawback in the rush to the city at present is the lack of house room. We know of several families who are waiting to come here, as soon as they can get houses.

In the fall of the same year the situation was still more acute as the *Daily True Democrat* indicates: "One hundred and seventy-five non-residents of Cleveland applied in Cleveland for houses to rent but only ten houses were available." To the very end of the period the situation remained serious. In March, 1853, the same paper states the case succinctly: "There was never so great a demand for houses as at present. Well-built dwellings are eagerly sought for, and bring an enormous rent."

Not surprisingly the old residential area northwest of the Square was quickly outgrown. Many of the finest residences invaded Lake Avenue, pushing eastward toward Clinton Square. The Public Square likewise continued to attract residences. In 1835 it was almost surrounded by private dwellings to judge by a slight pencil sketch by Leonard Case in that year which pictures the east and south sides of the Square closely built up with houses. This residential character of the Public Square remained until nearly mid-century.

As the population increased it became necessary to open new residential areas. Newspaper accounts show that the movement was toward the southeast with Pittsburgh and Prospect Streets forming new residential centers. It is also at this time that Euclid Avenue began its illustrious career as an avenue of fine homes. The Western Reserve Historical Society has an interesting collage, made from memory at a later date, which records this beginning in 1846-47. It shows an almost unbroken row of houses from the Square to Muirson Street (East 12th), many of them of considerable pretention (Figure 19).

This expansion of the residential district is borne out by the dates and locations of some of the famous early residences. It has been seen that Alfred Kelley's brick house was in the original residential district in 1817 at Lake and Water Streets. In 1824 the Case residence invaded the Square, followed by the Lemen house in 1829. This trend continued with the Winslow and Crittenden houses in 1832 and 1833. Shortly thereafter Euclid Avenue became a favorite locality. Cowles built there in 1833 and many followed suit, as the Schultze drawing reveals. One of the most pretentious houses on Euclid before mid-century was that of Henry Payne in 1849. Meantime Superior became fashionable. The May house at Superior and Erie was built in 1840. Woodland for a time in this period became a fashionable district also. Gaylord built there in 1836 and Harvey Rice in 1840. By the 1850's Prospect and Euclid were solidly built with residences well beyond the line of Erie Street, with a scattering of houses still farther east.

The churches and schools followed this migration of the residential areas to the east and south. Before 1830 the northwest quadrant of the town was the site of the Academy, and the only village church. In the 1830's the Square was chosen for new churches, in the 1840's Erie and Huron Streets and in the 1850's Euclid and Superior Streets to the east. The new schools which were erected in the 1840's were located in this same sector. Thus as the residential areas moved eastward and southeastward the schools and churches perforce followed.

The character of these better residential areas may be seen in a view of Euclid Avenue near Erie Street (Figure 20). Though this photograph dates from the 1860's the houses in most cases were built in the canal era and the pattern of the street development was set as early as the late 1840's. In contrast to the simple wooden-frame houses established in large plots or open fields which characterized

Public Sq.

B. J. Williamson
Mrs. S. Williamson School

Wm. Benedict

F. Dow

Geo H. Benedict

S. J. Andrews

Topping
S. R. Hutchinson

Wm Williams

C.W. Hazard's
Carpenter Shop

J. W. Morse

Euclid

Figure 19. Plan of Euclid Avenue in 1846.

Figure 20. Euclid Avenue, c.1865.

the town recorded by Thomas Whelpley, a sophisticated city district appears here. The houses are all of masonry or brick, and of two or more stories in height. They are set well back from the street, providing a generous yard inside the iron fences, but they are now closely spaced at equal distances from one another. The facades form a single straight line, giving the street a dignified air as a whole. With due allowance for the minor improvements which may have been effected between 1854 and the date of this photograph, it is clear that by the end of the canal period Cleveland had attained a gracious and even somewhat pretentious residential district commensurate with the prosperity of her enterprising merchants. As the old residential area northwest of the Square gave way to the invading business buildings, new and more imposing streets of fine homes developed to the east, each centered around its community church and near the neighborhood school.

While the residential areas were thus moving east and south and the builders were sorely pressed to keep pace with the mounting demand for houses, an equally ambitious development of commercial architecture was taking place in Cleveland. With the expansion of trade in the 1830's the number of warehouses and stores had to be multiplied, and brick replaced wood as a favorite material for this type of building after 1830.

The newspapers record a continuous enlargement of the town's commercial resources throughout this period in their recount of warehouses and stores constructed: 52 in 1835, 226 in 1845, are typical figures published by the press. Despite this volume of building complaints were constantly received that the facilities of the town were inadequate to the volume of business. Certainly this was a period of extraordinary expansion, judging by the builders' activities alone.

This volume of commercial buildings succeeded in changing the character of large areas almost completely. The changes were effected both by new construction and by the replacement of outworn buildings. The characteristic new building was a three or four-story brick structure and the first street to be invaded by the new type was, of course, Superior. By 1846 it had taken on a wholly new appearance. Comparison of the 1833 view of Superior by Whelpley with a drawing made by Henry Howe in 1846 indicates the sweeping nature of the change[51] (Figure 21). In the earlier print the buildings which lined the street had the character of private dwellings. They were of wooden construction with end-gables facing the street and on an average were two floors in height. By 1846, as Howe's drawing reveals, almost no remnants of this style of building remained. The street was then flanked by three and four-story square blocks, built closely together on the very edge of the sidewalk. In a word, Superior had become the characteristic mercantile street of the American city, a radical change to have taken place in less than two decades.

Though the street appears to be completely lined with buildings in this print, the process continued throughout this period. When open spaces were no longer available, finer buildings replaced outmoded ones and the destructive fires which at frequent intervals devastated large areas of the town hastened the transformation. With a view to curtailing the loss from fire the village leaders enacted at an early date the first piece of zoning legislation to find its way into the records. An editorial in the *Whig* on August 5, 1835, states that "the village corporation has passed an ordinance prohibiting the erection of wooden buildings on Superior Street." This law, with the inadequacy of fire-fighting equipment available at the time, hastened the transformation of the commercial district. Each wooden building destroyed gave way to a brick structure, until by mid-century only remnants of the older frame buildings remained.

A photograph of the south side of Superior looking west, taken in the early 1860's, reveals several stages of this revolutionary process (Figure 22). The highest building at the

Figure 21.
Superior Street in 1846.

Figure 22.
Superior Street, c.1860.

Figure 23.
Northrop & Spangler Block.

Figure 24.
Ontario Street, c.1858.

Figure 25.
Bank Street, c.1866.

center of this block was completed after 1860, but the remaining ones on each side date from the canal period. To the right of the Baldwin block is the three-story remnant of the inflammable wooden buildings of an earlier age. The general character of the street remains essentially that recorded by Howe in 1846. These plain three-story brick blocks seem hardly to justify the newspapers' designation of "elegant" which appears so frequently in their notices of new buildings. Before the end of the canal period, however, a few buildings of more distinction appear and give to certain sections of the street a somewhat greater dignity. A second view of Superior, adjacent to the Square, shows one of the best of these, the Northrop and Spangler (later Harrison) Block which was faced with cut stone and completed in 1853 (Figure 23). By such improvements the leading commercial street of town gradually acquired a more stable and impressive, if somewhat bleak appearance.

Superior Street had been the center of the retail trade ever since commerce became a factor in Cleveland and the transformation of these decades naturally was most striking there. A second center was early established, however, as soon as the town extended southward across Superior and branched out to the Southeast. The earliest building there was the Farmers' Block erected in 1836, but it was nearly mid-century before this new business section began to thrive. On November 7, 1848, the *Daily True Democrat* stated:

> We are glad to see business branching off from Superior Street where the excessive rents fatten landlords whilst they impoverish tenants. A good grocery, or a store of almost any kind, will make more money, and sell cheaper off Superior Street than on it.

The same editorial goes on to say, on a note of optimism:

> We notice that business is fast centering around the Market [Ontario Street]. Several buildings have recently been erected in that neighborhood and more will soon be required for business purposes.

Once well started by such new buildings this area continued to advance as a mercantile section and by the end of the period this region, like Superior Street, had attained the physical character of a retail district.

Ontario Street had not, however, achieved the same degree of "elegance" in its commercial buildings. A photograph of the street looking south from the Public Square probably taken in the late 1850's shows that the rather bald square blocks erected in these years were still interspersed with older wooden buildings (Figure 24).

This secondary center notwithstanding, Superior was too well entrenched to relinquish leadership. No sooner was the main street itself completely flanked by stores than the cross streets began to be rebuilt for business purposes. Retail establishments gradually invaded the district north of Superior, driving before them the old residences in the area. Frequent notices in the newspapers of the early 1850's mark the progress of the retail district northward toward the lake. On July 22, 1852, the *Daily True Democrat* made a pertinent prediction:

> Henry Wick will commence in a few days a brick block on the east side of Seneca St. north of the City Hotel. It will be 60 feet front, 60 feet deep, and three stories high. Bank St. will soon be built up. The next business street will necessarily be Seneca St., which we expect to see occupied with elegant brick blocks within three years.

Water Street had gradually been given over to business, and in 1853 a wholesale face-lifting operation there was announced by the same paper:

> There will be extensive improvements on Water St. this season. Fourteen brick buildings will probably be roofed before next fall. These are all between the Franklin block [Superior Street] and St. Clair, on the west side of Water St. All these buildings will be appropriated to business purposes

and every room not already taken, will be engaged before they are ready to use.

With the retail district driving northward at such a rate, it is not surprising that by the end of the canal period almost the entire northwest quadrant of the city was devoted to business houses. Step by step the old homes of the original residential area were pushed northward until in 1854 only a fringe of houses remained clinging precariously to the lakeshore.

These streets north of Superior were almost entirely commercial by 1854. In appearance they differ in no important particular from Superior Street itself. A view of Bank Street taken after 1866, but showing buildings of which all but one were at least ten years old at that date, shows the same ingredients (Figure 25). As the newspaper accounts indicate, they had been built by private capital for business purposes and were inspired primarily by the profit motive. Hence they were built close together and covered all space to the sidewalk line, leaving no room for planting in front or between the buildings. Then, too, as the area was one of competitive business, so the buildings compete for attention. Each structure is individual in style and does not attempt to accommodate its design to that of its neighbors. This is, of course, the character of commercial areas in most American cities to the present day. The system had its roots in these enterprising decades toward mid-century when the builders were less concerned with good design than with commercial prosperity.

The appetite of retail business for new locations was omnivorous. Toward mid-century the Public Square itself began to succumb. The progress of commercialization of the civic center was noted by the press in the period 1851 to 1854, a short three years which was sufficient to transform the Square. On March 14, 1854, the *Forest City Democrat* announced the approaching completion of the process: "The 'Old Stone Cottage' [Lemen House, built 1829] is being torn down, its site to be occupied by a brick block. The

entire Square will soon be surrounded by such buildings." The *Leader,* rejoices in the new building:

> In viewing the many improvements made this season not one has risen more like magic than the imposing and elegant brick block of four stories erected by Dr. H. L. Hoffman on the northeast corner of the Public Square and Superior St. It is divided into eight stores on the first floor and 13 rooms in each of the stories above.

By the end of this period, then, the retail district had spread from its center at Superior Street, northward toward the lake, across to Ontario where a second focal center developed and finally eastward to enclose the Public Square. Except for Superior Street itself, most of these gains were made at the expense of the residential areas in each part of the city so invaded. In particular the whole character of the northwest sector, and of the circumference of the Public Square, was completely changed. Outposts of the retail district were likewise established in the preponderately wholesale and warehouse areas along the river, on River and Canal Streets and on Merwin Street in Cleveland Centre.

The hotel business was greatly expanded in these same years. And just as the schools and churches followed the spread of the residential areas, so the hotels were stimulated by the expansion of business. As Superior Street remained the nucleus of this trade, despite its lateral extension, so the largest and most pretentious hotels were built along the length of this street. The increase between 1830 and 1854 was truly phenomenal. It was an exceptional year which passed without a new hotel being erected or an old one remodelled or improved. Aside from minor changes in the old Cleveland House at the Square, the first important addition to Superior Street was the American House, which arose opposite the Franklin House in 1837. In the 1840's the numbers multiplied, as did the retail trade which fostered them. In 1844 Philo Scovill completely rebuilt the Franklin

House, enlarging it in the process to many times its former capacity. Hardly was this task completed than the largest hotel yet to grace the city was started next door. This was the famous Weddell House, and such was the pressure of business that by 1853 this already spacious hotel was doubled in size by extensive additions on Bank and Centre Streets. Meantime at the river end of Superior Street the New England Hotel was built in the year of 1846-1847. Nor was this all. The old Cleveland House at Superior on the Square had burned in 1845 and in 1847 a new hotel and business block replaced it, under the title of the Dunham House. By 1850 a wing fronting on the Square was likewise added to this hotel. In 1852 it was once more enlarged and, in changing hands, became known as the Forest City House. By the end of this period Superior Street could boast no less than five flourishing hotels within the three blocks between the Square and the river, all of them comparatively new and all of considerable size. Only one important hotel was built off Superior at this time. The Angier House on the corner of Bank and St. Clair came into being just at the end of this period in 1852-54, thus following closely in the footsteps of the migrating business district. A number of smaller hotels were, of course, to be found in other parts of the retail zone. In all cases these closely followed the pattern of expansion of the retail district.

The changes which most materially effected the character of Cleveland before 1854 were produced by the development of the retail business district. Under its impetus large areas took on a new complexion which, with minor additions and modifications, has lasted to the present day. But in addition, there were two other contemporary developments which effected the appearance of the town, this time in the restricted area of the flats along the river. These were the development first of wholesale houses and secondly of small industrial establishments during these same years. Of these the enlargement of wholesale business was easily the more significant. Until the advent of the railroads and of Lake Superior iron ores, Cleveland's prosperity rested upon trade. It was first of all a shipping point and mercantile center. Only after mid-century did industry become an effective factor in shaping the town.

The goods which comprised the bulk of this trade reached Cleveland by way of the lakes or the canal. The wholesale district therefore was located on the water front where warehouses, piers, docks, and commission houses multiplied. River Street from the lake to Superior Lane, and Merwin Street which flanked the stream in Cleveland Centre were bordered by these wholesale establishments. Paralleling these streets an unbroken line of wharves was built adjacent to the river itself and this, which became known as Dock Street (vacated), was in turn lined by warehouses. In a few instances neighboring streets were put to use as the shipping business increased, but the river front itself remained the important wholesale center throughout this period. A large lithograph of Cleveland in 1853, picturing the town as seen from the west side of the river, shows clearly what has happened (Figure 26). A comparison of this print with the view of 1833, which shows roughly the same area, provides a measure of the expansion of wholesale trade. During the intervening decades the open spaces between warehouses were filled in by buildings right to the water's edge as the demand for warehouse space multiplied. In the pervading enthusiasm for mercantile expansion, on which after all the prosperity of the town rested, no thought was given to other possible uses of the water front. Business succeeded in pre-empting the whole river bank and space was allocated neither to residential nor to recreational uses. As early, then, as 1853 the choice sites along the river were closed to the public and the foundations laid for the domination of the

Figure 26. View of Cleveland from the west in 1853.

whole river valley by industry and trade, a condition which characterizes the area at the present day.

The years of expansion which transformed Cleveland from a rural village to a mercantile city not only redesigned the town, but introduced for the first time the need for public services and utilities. In the sparsely-populated village of 1833 dirt roads without sidewalks served well enough the transportation needs of the small population. The town pump and private wells supplied a sufficient water supply. Street lights were unheard of and unnecessary and the Public Square was all the park required in a village surrounded by open fields. Long before 1854, however, the multiplying population, the crowded streets and overbuilt lots, made new demands. The condition of the dirt roads deteriorated rapidly with the increase in wheeled traffic. Mud and dust created nuisances for driver and pedestrian alike. A chorus of protest arose against mud holes and debris, against live stock in the streets and in the Public Square. There was widespread demand for recreation areas and for a more adequate water supply. Street lights became imperative. As early as 1836 the *Herald* printed frequent notices requesting sidewalks on Superior, and in the same year a concerted effort was first made to improve the streets by grading. In 1840 the first culverts were dug in the main streets and reports of constant repairs were printed in the newspapers in these years. As the population increased and business thrived, the traffic of heavy wagons frustrated the best efforts of the road menders. In an effort to meet the difficulty a sort of poll tax of two days' work was exacted from each resident of town. The Western Reserve Historical Society preserves this interesting notice:[52]

> Mr. A. Colman. You are hereby notified to attend on the 2 & 3 days of August, 1844, in St. Clair Street, front of the Academy, in the City of Cleveland, at the hour of seven o'clock, in the forenoon, with a good and sufficient Shovel, to perform the two days labor required of you by law.
>
> John Wills. Street Supervisor of the City of Cleveland.

Each spring, however, the work of the previous year was undone as the frost worked out of the ground. The dirt streets became clogged with mud and, as the mire dried, it was replaced by dust. On July 29, 1848, the *Daily True Democrat* laments: "Superior Street is like a 'trouble sea' — and it needs purifying especially of hog holes." In April of the next year there is a different complaint in the same paper: "The dust is intolerable. If that sprinkler is not brought out we will endeavor to kick up a fuss generally." To the end of the canal period there is repeated reference in both facetious and irritated terms to the deplorable condition of streets and sidewalks.

It soon became apparent that the most conscientious efforts would be insufficient to maintain the dirt roads. Some more durable material for street surfacing became imperative. In the late 1830's the first, if very primitive, solution was tried on the roads beyond the outskirts of town. The *Herald* on March 26, 1845, gives a contemporary description of these planked roads as used in the countryside:

> They [the planks] were laid eight years ago and are 16 feet long and 3 inches thick, on four sills four inches square, fastened by one spike in each of the planks.

In the 1840's these were adapted to the city streets, and an increasing number of references were made in the newspapers after 1846 to the extension of planked roads across the main arteries of the city.

These wooden surfaces which had been hailed with so much enthusiasm as the solution to all traffic problems soon were found to be inadequate. They required constant repair as the planks wore through under the wheels of stages and freight-wagons and as the wood rotted out. In 1843 agitation commenced to pave Superior Street with stone because of "the wretched and frequently impassable condition" of that main thoroughfare, to quote the *Herald* for November 20. In 1845 stone pavement was again demanded because of less upkeep and replacement from rot. Very little progress was made, however, and on February 27, 1849, the *Daily True Democrat* is bitter about the situation: "There has never been one foot of sidewalk flagging done at the expense of the city, and there is not one rod of pavement in the city." Perhaps in response to such pressure some action was taken, for in the next year part of Superior was paved with stone and a number of streets in the following years were treated with gravel. It was not until the 1860's, however, that the wood-block paving known as Nicholson pavement came into general use and only in the 1870's did any of the modern paving methods appear.[53] Pedestrians were treated somewhat better, as the city council passed an ordinance in 1854 compelling property owners to pave their sidewalks.

The drainage of streets, of whatever type of surface, was not solved by the primitive culverts installed during these decades. Only at the end of this period, however, was a forthright solution of the problem determined upon. On August 10, 1853, the *Leader* published the first notice that more satisfactory installations were being undertaken:

> The route of the city sewers for the drainage of the eastern part of the city has been completed. The total estimated cost of the whole line of sewers is $46,274.

The work was extended as rapidly as finances permitted during 1853 and the following years. At best the efforts of this generation served barely to keep ahead of the mounting problems of street repair and maintenance created by the increasing traffic and the growing population. Under the pressures of public opinion the period before 1854 saw only the first steps taken toward a solution of the continuing problem.

One interesting sidelight on the nature of the problems fostered by expansion is given by this notice in the *Daily True Democrat* on June 23, 1848: "The city council last night adopted a resolution authorizing the supervisor to place signs on the corners of various streets." The town obviously was outgrowing that stage of infancy when its every house and street was familiar to each of its inhabitants.

It was in this period likewise, that public utilities first came into being. The water supplied by wells continued to serve the residential districts, but in the center of town a more generous supply was found necessary. In 1846 there were two small reservoirs within the city, one at Bond and Superior Streets, and a second at the corner of Bank and Lake. Three years later a much larger one was projected and arrangements made to supply the center of town with running water. The *Daily True Democrat* gives a description of this system on August 4, 1849:

> On March 18 operations were commenced on Meadow, near Light St. The tank built of brick, which was completed July 30, is 50 feet in diameter, extends 17 feet into the ground, is capable of holding 250,000 gallons of water. Pipes are now being laid in all business streets and should be ready for use in November.

This supply, small as it may seem in comparison to modern arrangements, proved sufficient for some years, and pipes were extended to the streets adjacent to the center of town in ensuing decades.

The second public utility also had its start in the canal period. On April 4, 1849, the *Daily True Democrat* served notice of the intention:

> A Gas Company was chartered by the late Legislature, in this city, and a contract has been entered into by the company, with John Jeffrey and Co., for the construction of Gas Works and laying of pipes etc., work to be completed by 1st of Jan., 1850.

The same paper noted that: "Mr. Jeffrey is a business man of the right sort of energy." An accurate estimate it would seem inasmuch as: "The gas lights along the principal streets of our city are to be ready for use by the middle of November." On the 28th of September the project was described in some detail:

> An appropriation not exceeding $3200 for the purposes of lighting the City of Cleveland with gas has been made by the city council. The following are the streets to be lighted this fall: Superior St. from the river to Erie Street; Public Square around to the market; Water St. from Superior St. to Bath St.; Merwin St. from Superior to Stone Pier; and Bank St. from Superior St. to Bath St. The lamps will be placed 200 feet apart and will completely illuminate the streets as each light will be equal to ten sperm candles and will cast a shadow 300 feet away.

With this modest beginning installed and in operation by December 8, the era of lighted streets came to Cleveland. In the next years the service was greatly extended both to new streets and also to buildings adjacent to the gas lines.

Less success met the demand for lands to be set aside for public use. In the village of the 1830's when each lot was generous and the open fields crowded in upon the residential section, there was little enough need for more extensive parks than the Public Square. Nevertheless, with a vision which was rare indeed, some civic minded person foresaw a growing need for publicly controlled recreation areas. On May 13, 1835, this notice was published in the *Whig*:

> A petition will be presented to the Board of Trustees for Cleveland Village, at their first meeting after 1st July next — praying that a Public Square may be opened and established — to comprise the ground between Superior and St. Clair, Erie and Bond St.

At the time of this petition the area in question was just beginning to be claimed as a residential district. The ground could have been obtained at a minimum price and a fine centrally located park reserved for the city. The council failed to see the advantages and the petition was denied.

This was to become the pattern for the entire period of mercantile expansion. Despite repeated demands by the public and editorial comment at frequent intervals, it was not until 1865 that public funds were allocated to parks.

In two short decades then, Cleveland had been redesigned in all its parts. Thanks largely to the prosperity occasioned by mercantile enterprise, the river front had become crowded with warehouses and stock piles, the retail district had changed radically in appearance and spread laterally at the expense of the residential areas. The mounting population had overridden the town limits several times and a network of new streets had been created and lined with prosperous homes to accommodate the increase. The responsibilities of a city, calling for care of streets and the provision of utilities and parks, had been thrust upon the village. In this process an almost completely new town had been brought into being.

In no small part, too, the changed appearance of the town was the result of the new character of its individual buildings. As prosperity was created by the expanding mercantile activity, investment in finer buildings became possible. The merchants soon realized the prestige value of well-designed business blocks and the hotels, as well, vied with one another to produce more attractive designs. When the older churches were outgrown, the congregations were housed in larger and handsomer buildings, and particularly in the residential areas pride of ownership demanded more solid houses and more elaborate styling.

Several innovations in architectural practice made these accomplishments possible. In fact, in order to fulfill the aspirations of the city on architectural lines something of a revolution took place in the building arts before 1854. New materials of a finer and more durable quality became practical by reason of the invention of new power tools for their shaping, and a younger generation of better trained craftsmen and designers emerged. Architecturally the western community was growing up and partaking of the national character in the design of its buildings.

The most radical change in the building materials after 1830 was the decline in the importance of wood. The trend was clearly in favor of other materials. Wood was, for one thing, less abundant. Land clearing, both in the town itself and in the adjacent countryside as well, had created shortages where plethora had existed only a few years before. Also, as has been seen, more nearly fireproof construction was encouraged wherever possible. But still more important perhaps was the new taste for more monumental forms which demanded the solidity and scale which masonry could best achieve. Under these circumstances the wooden building gradually gave way first to brick and then to stone. The clay which abounded in the country made brick a cheap and practical commodity. By 1850 the retail district in particular was dominated by this material, and many of the churches, schools and some of the finest residences were built of brick.[54]

Stone was at first used more sparingly. Though popular for details of decorative trim and foundations as early as the second Court House of 1828, it was an expensive material because of the difficulties it presented to the craftsman and few buildings of cut stone are found until late in the canal period. As more efficient methods of cutting the Berea sandstone became available, however, this material grew in favor and was used as facing on many of the more expensive buildings before mid-century. An occasional building was constructed entirely of stone.

Several manufactured materials were introduced in small quantities toward the end of the canal period. Due to the presence of low grade coal and iron in central Ohio, a small quantity of iron was available after the canals came into operation. This was used largely for decorative purposes until the late 1850's when the Superior hematites began to arrive in quantity in Cleveland and made possible the use of iron for structural forms. The canals likewise permitted the importation of glass from Pittsburgh, and the size of windows was increased, especially in the mercantile buildings. Finally, at the very end of the canal period a synthetic material, the first of its kind to appear in Cleveland, was advertised in the newspapers and actually put to use. This was an "artificial sandstone," and at least two buildings were faced with this as a substitute for stone before the end of the decade.

Along with these changes in materials a number of technological improvements were introduced before 1854. The most important of these was the recently invented "balloon frame," developed in Chicago in 1832. This was a method of building with small dimension timbers which were toe-nailed in place, eliminating the laborious process of cutting the mortise and tenon by hand. The whole method of construction in wood was revolutionized by this process. There is direct evidence that this efficient method of construction in wood was being used in Cleveland in the 1840's as will be seen. In view of the mushroom growth of the town in these decades, calling for a tremendous volume of building, this was an event of no small importance.

At the same time new power-driven tools were being introduced for the shaping of materials. A typical such invention was a lath-cutting machine which practically eliminated the laborious process of sawing out lath by hand. According to its description in the *Herald* on May 16, 1846, this machine was capable of transforming the rough log into lath at the rate of 115 to 130 a minute. This process, bordering on the mass production methods of more modern times, must have proved a boon to the hard-pressed builders in this period of expansion.

As far as the effect upon the architectural character of the period is concerned, probably the most significant of these power tools was a stone-dressing machine. Attention is first called to this invention by the *Daily True Democrat* on October 19, 1848:

An invention for cutting stone is in operation in New Haven, which dresses down stone at the rate of a square foot in from one to two minutes, with 2 attendants only, and with a limited amount of steam power doing the labor of more than a hundred men. There's said to be no mistake in the thing; and if so, it promises to make stone supersede brick, and revolutionize entirely our mode of building.

Though the effects of this tool were not quite so revolutionary as the newspaper predicted, it did succeed in providing larger quantities of stone at lower cost. It was introduced at Cleveland within a few years and was advertised by the *Daily True Democrat* in August, 1853:

The Cleveland Stone-Dressing Co.'s quarry is in Independence. Sandstone of this quarry is so excellent that there is a large and growing demand for it for exportation, east, west, and north. The company's yard and workshops for 'dressing' this stone are in Ohio City, near the old river bed, and command all the desirable facilities of water and land communications. The cutting machine now operated by the company sweeps a surface three and a half feet by ten, and, with the aid of five men, who need not possess much mechanical dexterity, does the same amount of work as 50 experts using the ordinary or old process, and does it better. The power needed to drive this is some five-horse.

The effect of this labor-saving machine on the architecture of Cleveland was almost immediate. It now became practicable to build whole buildings, and face others, with the more durable and handsomer material. The trend is pointed out by the *Daiy True Democrat* in August, 1853:

Builders are beginning to exhibit a decided partiality to stone fronts. In our opinion they are a great improvement. Besides excelling in beauty, they are much more durable and give a finished, elegant appearance to a building, that no other kind of stone can do.

In the next few years there were frequent references to the increasing use of stone and marble in building. As a result,

by the time of the Civil War the brick business block was almost obsolete in the center of retail Cleveland, and the churches and even the private residence were able to afford the "luxury" material.

The first development of a partially synthetic material was the product of the very end of this period. A notice in the *Leader* describes this experimental product:

We went into the yard back of Bennett House yesterday where Boyer and Sawyer are making their new kind of brick called 'Artificial Sandstone'. Some points about this new material are worthy of note. It furnishes a building material easily and quickly made up into any desired form, such as brick, by pressing it into a die and permitting it to harden, and it is said to subsequently become as hard as granite itself. A thin cement is used to unite the block making the whole mass like a solid rock. The bricks are made hollow by a core in the die so that when laid in the wall the air communicates through it from top to bottom, thus securing a perfectly dry wall. The materials of which the bricks are made are the cheapest and most common; viz: sand and quick lime. They can be made any color desired by mixing paint with the components.

This promising material, which from the description sounds very much like the forerunner of contemporary concrete block, was promptly put to use. The same paper announced in September of that same year of 1855 that: "The new building on the west side of the Square above the Bennett House is to be faced with the new sand brick."

In the matter, then, of techniques and materials the canal period in Cleveland produced some interesting labor-saving devices which permitted the designing of more elaborate buildings, and at the same time the first experiments with synthetic materials were conducted. Both developments were significant harbingers of the trends of later decades.

The constructive use of these new techniques and materials called for a higher degree of skill on the part of the designers. The carpenter-craftsmen of the older tradition could no longer cope successfully with the problems of large-scale buildings of fine materials and mature architectural style. As the techniques became more complex and the styles more sophisticated, the training and experience of the builders had to keep pace. To solve the problem, the services of eastern architects were demanded in a few instances. A great majority of the buildings were, however, built by local men who had succeeded in making the necessary adjustments to the new conditions. These men were usually artisans who had come up from the ranks of carpenters and masons, turning to design as soon as their experience and ambition permitted. A typical example of such an evolution was the career of Charles W. Heard. He was listed in the *Directory* of 1837-1838 as a carpenter and joiner, but in 1845-1846 he is self-styled as a "master builder." In the next year he became associated with W. J. Warner, a mason, and organized a contracting business on an enlarged basis. In 1850, without relinquishing his association with Warner, he is listed as an "architect" in the firm of Heard and Porter, and in 1853 the *Directory* again reads "Heard and Porter, architects and builders." This evolution is indicative. Charles W. Heard was by training a carpenter. In this guise he was undoubtedly well occupied in the 1830's keeping pace with the demands for the frame structures which characterized that decade. As his skill and experience and the volume of his output increased, he assumed direction of a corps of assistants and took the title of master builder. At this time, however, wood construction was being supplemented by brick and stone, and Heard promptly associated himself with a mason to maintain his progress. This firm produced the jail in 1841, one of the earliest stone buildings in town. By 1850 Heard had more and more concentrated upon the designing end of the firm's business, and since this took a large part of his time, he brought a master-builder, S. J. Porter, into the firm to supervise construction. In this and subsequent years the experience and ability of this team produced a large number of the most advanced buildings in Cleveland. The name of

Heard and Porter is associated with the Second Presbyterian Church, St. Paul's Church and the High School, among many others. Thus the leading firm of architects, serving both as designers and builders in the canal period, arose from the trades and created the most ambitious buildings in Cleveland to that date.

Such men as Charles W. Heard never had, at any stage of their careers, the professional training available to architects in the east or in Europe. Their knowledge of materials and their skill in construction were alike the product of long years of actual experience in the building trades. This experience served them well as far as construction was concerned. It was sufficient to produce the majority of the residences in the town, the average commercial block or warehouse, and the smaller hotels. These buildings were without pretensions to official "style," were in fact for the most part architecturally nondescript. A growing percentage of the buildings erected in the canal period, on the other hand, aspired to greater architectural dignity. The new hotels and a few of the better business blocks, the latest schools, and in particular the churches and residences of the elite of Cleveland were designed with this end in view. The experience of these builders was in itself insufficient to meet this new demand. They were not qualified by training to design Greek columns, Gothic arches, nor Renaissance brackets. They were provincial men without firsthand experience with the fashions of the east, much less with those of Europe. In order, therefore, to endow their finer buildings with the architectural character their patrons demanded they were driven to other sources. This need was supplied in part by the carpenters' manuals.

The use of such manuals as a source of style was a firmly established practice. Throughout almost the whole course of American architecture these volumes, for the most part British publications, had been used by the carpenters, both amateur and professional, as a source for their designs. Just before the turn of the century the first American pattern book appeared, that of Asher Benjamin in 1796, and thereafter the number increased rapidly.[55] By the canal period in Cleveland a great variety of such books, English as well as American, were at hand to guide the builder in his choice of architectural forms. Most of them were composed by competently trained architects, such as Benjamin, Minard Lafever and Richard Upjohn, though a few were less professional in quality. But even the best of them were seldom sufficiently detailed to supply the builder with a complete and accurate guide. Characteristically, such a volume would include some pages of rhetoric on the history of architecture and the philosophy of the art of building. Many pages of general instructions would follow which were of value as guiding principles but did not provide the carpenter with detailed information. These would be interspersed with small sketches of suggested buildings, sometimes accompanied by a floor plan, which were more often than not quite inadequate for use as a pattern for a finished building. Nothing approaching the blueprints required to complete a building with accuracy was provided. The only illustrations drawn to scale and with the detail necessary to serve as patterns were the ornamental forms appropriate to the style presented.

As a result of these limitations, the pattern books were used by the builders in a very free manner. Since it was practically impossible to reproduce on the ground a building so summarily sketched, there are few instances of exact copies. Rather the general character of the style would be followed and ornamental details lifted from the scale drawings where appropriate. The adaptations of the successive styles offered by these manuals were, therefore, free and haphazard, and allowed for a considerable degree of initiative on the part of the builder.

Nonetheless, the trends of taste were guided largely by these manuals. As one style succeeded another in the pattern books, it appeared on the streets of Cleveland. In the absence of formal stylistic training among the builders, the carpenter's handbooks helped to engender the architectural fashions of the period.

There was a second equally important factor which shaped the architectural character of Cleveland. This was the period of the maturing of the midwest, which to this time had been largely a frontier society. It was developing to a point at which it could take an active part in the national culture and the architectural forms of such towns as Cleveland shared in the formation of national styles. The common idioms which developed before the Civil War were to be found in the cities just east of the Mississippi almost as soon as they were making their appearance in the more sophisticated cultural centers farther east. As provincialism diminished the forms being produced by such innovators as Isaiah Rogers, Ithiel Town and Richard Upjohn were adapted to Western condition, exchanged between western centers of culture, and permeated the central states. To understand the evolution of taste in Cleveland, therefore, frequent reference must be made to the national idioms and to the work of stylistic leaders which these decades developed.

The period between 1830 and 1850 was one of the most fruitful in the history of American architecture. It was motivated in large part by the ideals which had their beginnings in the Federal style. Despite its variety, the latter had sought a harmonious and unified architectural form with American connotations and had produced its finest monuments in the official buildings in the cultural centers of the east. The Greek Revival was the successor of the Federal style and more nearly succeeded in establishing a national style than any comparable period in American art. With comparatively minor regional differences it spread across the country with the tides of emigration and, as it were, grew up with the expanding culture of the opening west.

The seeds of the Greek Revival style had been planted by Benjamin Latrobe at the turn of the century, and it was his pupils who gave it mature form. William Strickland in particular created an elegant and refined type of public building dominated by Greek orders and in the north Ithiel Town, Isaiah Rogers and Ammi B. Young developed monumental forms with Greek detail. In the work of George Hadfield among others a dignified domestic architecture emerged in Greek dress. The interest in Greek detail quickly reached the carpenters' manuals and in the publications of Benjamin and those of Minard Lafever crisp drawings of the Greek orders began to appear. From such sources there developed in the 1830's a refined and versatile vernacular design on a domestic scale which blanketed the country.

Because it was felt that the Greek forms were particularly appropriate to the American ideals, (and indeed the style had no comparable popularity in any other country), the Greek Revival persisted almost until the Civil War. During its reign it expressed the desire for national independence and reflected the enthusiasm for classical culture which characterized the period.

The same period, however, saw the beginnings of other tendencies in American design. Side by side with the development of the Greek Revival a variety of fashions emerged starting with the Gothic Revival. Largely literary in its inspiration, the interest in medieval forms opened the door to two tendencies which ultimately dominated American architecture: preoccupation with historical styles and the decline of structural soundness and forthright use of materials. Even in the work of leading practitioners of the Gothic Revival, such as Richard Upjohn and A. J. Davis, historicism tended to undermine the structural soundness of their buildings. The Gothic style became firmly implanted in religious architecture in the 1840's and produced for a brief period large numbers of "picturesque" designs in do-

mestic and public buildings. It opened the way for a variety of experiments in other foreign styles of the past. The stylistic evolution of such architects as Upjohn and the firm of Town and Davis reveals the eclectic character which dominated the period toward mid-century. This kaleidoscope was reflected in the manuals, as in those of Andrew J. Downing in 1842 and thereafter.

Only a small proportion of the total building of these decades had any official style in this sense. Many of the writers on architecture, headed by Horatio Greenough, insisted upon the importance of building which would be serviceable and indigenous in character. And in fact there began to emerge in the cities a large proportion of utilitarian structures: factories, warehouses, railroad stations, hotels and business blocks which were almost entirely without historic style at all. They were built by artisans to serve the manifold requirements of the commercial town and constituted a solid substratum of forthright building which retained the best of the indigenous tradition of the country.

The architecture of Cleveland, as part of a national development at this time, reflected these various phases of architectural taste in the period of the canals. In contrast to the earlier period in her architectural history, there were between 1830 and 1854 a large number of buildings with sound character, representing a variety of building types and a sequence of fashions. Several hotels and business blocks reflect the trend in commercial design; a few typical school buildings are worth analysis; many churches and private residences demonstrate the developing forms of the period.

One of the curiosities of the canal period in Cleveland is the fact that no important government building was erected. The only civic structure undertaken was a two-story jail, a quite unprepossessing affair of little architectural interest beyond the fact that it was of stone. The second Court

House, completed in 1828, was refurbished and painted in 1849 and continued to serve until 1858 when it gave way to a new building erected on a site north of the Square. The city government was served throughout this period by rooms located in one or another of the business buildings of the city. The first city hall was not built until the 1870's.

On the other hand, expanding trade and a growing population called for a large number of hotels and business buildings, as has already been seen, and some of these are of considerable interest. The first major hotel of the period was the American House on Superior Street almost opposite the end of Bank Street. It opened its doors to guests on January 1, 1838 (Figure 27). It took its architectural character from the fact that it occupied only the upper stories of Kellogg's Block and therefore had something in common with the commercial buildings in the city. Like the better business blocks it was a brick structure of five stories terminated by a cornice, but a finer design than was common in mercantile buildings was here attained, justifying in part its reputation as a "magnificent establishment." The level of each floor was marked on the facade by a horizontal string-course and the bays were divided by pilasters which provided a certain plasticity in the front elevation. In 1851 the design was given a central focal point by the addition, during an extensive remodelling which included a spacious lobby on the ground floor, of one of the first balconies to be supported by cast iron columns to appear in Cleveland. Unfortunately the only available print of the building in its remodelled state gives no adequate idea of the detail of this important innovation in the use of iron.

The new Franklin House was the second important hotel to appear on Superior Street (Figure 28). It was erected in 1844-45 by Philo Scovill as a replacement for the original hotel of the same name and its opening was announced by the *Herald* on May 30, 1845. A measure of the architectural progress made in Cleveland is provided by a comparison of the old and the new building. The three-story woodenframe building of 1825-26 (Figure 9) with its carpenter-designed features reminiscent of 18th-century New England was replaced by a brick building of four stories plus an attic. The ground floor which housed several stores was faced with brick pilasters and the center of the facade was recessed to provide an entrance at street level and a balcony on the second floor. These were supported by stone Doric columns and a simplified stone entablature. A triple string-course, likewise of stone, formed the crowning motive below and above the attic windows.

These two hotels have several features in common which were new to Cleveland design. The central porches which rise through the lower floors (projecting in the case of the American House and recessed on the Franklin) and the Greek motifs (a cornice on the American House and a Doric order on the Franklin) are elements of the Greek Revival style. They had been made popular by the well-known Tremont House in Boston, built in 1827-28 by Isaiah Rogers. Neither of the Cleveland buildings had the quality of the Boston hotel, but they are nonetheless direct evidence of the emergence, for the first time in Cleveland, of a new concept in the design of public buildings.

A year after the new Franklin was completed a towering neighbor arose next door to eclipse its fame. The Weddell House was to become one of the most illustrious of the hotels of Cleveland, and it caught the attention of the newspapers even before completion. The *Herald*, in November of 1846, thus described the plan of the building:

> The building is located at Superior and Bank Streets, the business center of the city. No public building in any other western cities [sic] equal Weddell House for size and convenience. The main building is 5 stories high. A 3 story annex has been added to accommodate servants and to serve as kitchen space. The entire building includes about 200 rooms. On the ground floor on Sup. side are a bank and four

Figure 28.
Second Franklin House, 1844-1845.

Figure 27.
American House after remodeling, after 1900.

Figure 29. Weddell House, c.1875.

Figure 31. Hoffman Block in 1880.

Figure 30. Weddell House during remodeling, c.1885.

stores. Two large law offices take up the Super. St. side of the second floor, while on the Bank St. side of that floor is a large dining hall. The Bank St. side of the ground floor includes a reading room, several parlors and 3 stores. The third floor is divided into living and bedroom suites, while the fourth floor, in addition to numerous living and bedroom suites, includes a large assembly room. The fifth floor consists of numerous bedrooms.

This description reveals that in the Weddell House, Cleveland had for the first time a hotel provided with a variety and size of public rooms approaching the luxury of the famous Tremont in Boston. The community was justly proud of the attainment, as this notice in the *Herald* on the date of its opening on June 30, 1847, indicates: "It is with some emotions of pride that we acknowledge that the Weddell House is now open for the reception of Guests."

Despite its size as originally built, the demand for accommodations was such that in 1853 a four-story extension on Bank Street and a wing on Center were added. It underwent several later refurnishings and, in the 1880's a complete remodelling including redesign of the windows on the facade and the enlargement of the fifth floor. In 1904 it was replaced by the present Rockefeller Building, although the four-story addition on Bank Street remained until 1961.

The appearance of the hotel as first built is preserved in Howe's drawing of Superior Street in 1846 (Figure 21). It was a looming, four-square structure of four and one-half floors like the adjacent Franklin House. Each floor in the new hotel was, however, several feet higher than in the Franklin, with the result that the Weddell towers well above its neighbor, an indication of the new taste for high ceilings which was to reach its climax in the mansard styles after the Civil War. The ground floor, which was largely given over to offices and stores, was faced with sandstone, while the main body of the building above was constructed of brick and trimmed with stone. This trim consisted of quoins at the corner of the building, stone lintels and sills at the doors and windows and in the crowning string-courses at the height of the wall. As described by the *Herald*, a recessed balcony was inset at the corner and supported by stone columns which rose through two floors. The octagonal cupola was developed in two stages above the roof and crowned by a small dome, quite inadequate to the bulk of the building below. Though an extensive building, particularly after the construction of its new wing, the Weddell House at this time was a severe design, especially in the treatment of the wall surfaces (Figure 29). This simple character of wall, as seen both here and in the Franklin House, was a significant American characteristic before mid-century which may be found in all utilitarian categories of building in many parts of the country. The recessed balcony of the Weddell on the other hand is supported by monumental Doric columns for which a source was available in one or another of the carpenter's manuals. Scale drawings of Doric columns, rendered in clear outlines, were published by Asher Benjamin, for example. Applied here as ornamental accessories to a building which has little other claim to any historical style they demonstrate the characteristic use to which these builders' guides were put.

A photograph of about 1885 which shows the Weddell House while in process of being extensively remodelled reveals many of the structural details[56] (Figure 30). With the roof removed and part of the Bank Street wall torn down, the fabric of the building is laid bare. It may be seen that the exterior walls of brick formed a thin shell which was cross-braced by dividing brick walls to stabilize the structure. These lateral walls were built up in pediment form to support the flattened gable roof, the marks of which remain on adjacent buildings on each flank. This gable was hidden by the parapet which crowned the outer walls so that it could not be seen from the street. All other structural parts of the building were of wood. The floors consisted of closely spaced joists which were carried by the outer brick walls. The partitions were built up of small dimension timbers toenailed in place. This is a system derived from the development of "balloon-frame" construction which had its beginning in the previous decade in Chicago. Here is clear evidence that this labor and expense-saving method of construction was replacing the older method in the buildings of Cleveland in the 1840's, a technological advance of prime importance in view of the volume of building which was necessary in these years.

As the views of the business streets have shown, the average commercial building at this time was a severely plain design in which utility and cheapness were primary considerations. The desire for a building with finer quality was felt toward the end of this period, however, and a few such buildings were erected in better materials and more sophisticated taste. The Hoffman Block may be numbered among these and was one of the early business buildings to invade the Public Square. It was raised on the site of the Lemen House in 1854, a symptom of the changing character of the civic center. It was a four-story structure which housed stores at the ground level and offices above, and was considered a very fine and elegant building at the time. The photographs of it, taken at a later date when it had become dirty and shabby, hardly seem to justify this high esteem. To judge from one dated in the 1880's, the Hoffman Block was a rather plain building of brick, dominated as was usual by rows of windows (Figure 31). Some architectural dignity was achieved, however, by enlarging the windows at the central axis of the building and by surmounting each window by a small cornice drawn in a flattened arc. This motive was repeated under the projecting cornice at the height of the wall to produce a curiously scalloped architrave. A series of brackets supported the cornice above. Added to the otherwise severe facade characteristic of

mercantile structures to this time these details seem to reflect the increasing sophistication to be found after 1850.

The Northrop and Spangler Block, completed in 1853, was the most pretentious business building of its day (Figure 23). Though of only four floors, like its neighbors, it towered above them and had a better quality which set it apart from the rest of Superior Street near the Square. It was one of the first mercantile buildings to be faced with cut stone, a product of the new power-operated machines so recently put into use in Cleveland, and the smooth finish and sharp detail added considerably to the quality of the building. The design is quite competent. The ground floor is accented by a string-course and the crown of the building by a solid cornice of heavy Greek dentils. Each window is crowned by a narrow cornice in high relief creating an insistent rhythm across the facade. These are sharply defined, well related to the areas of smooth wall surface, and Greek in type. By comparison to the unambitious blocks so common at this time, this was a tasteful and impressive building which compares favorably to the better utilitarian designs being produced in other large commercial centers such as New York City or Boston.

Together with the hotels, these commercial buildings gave the retail districts of town their character. By 1854 the business areas of Cleveland were on their way to attaining a fairly high standard of commercial architecture. Most of them had the structural simplicity and sharp detail which were the best features of American utilitarian building in these decades.

Much the same rudimentary form dominated the public schools before 1854. The motive of economy was a primary factor here and the designs were kept as simple as possible, with a few architectural embellishments added when funds permitted. It is a curious fact that, despite the rapid growth of population after 1830, the old Academy remained the only building erected at public expense for school purposes for a full decade. Private schools took up the burden of the education of children in Cleveland until public pressure forced the authorities to set aside funds and construct two new buildings in 1840.[57] In 1845 a third was constructed, followed by a fourth in 1847. These were all alike, built after a single set of plans and at an expenditure of $3500 apiece. An amusing and indicative sidelight on the methods of the period is given by this advertisement in the *Herald and Gazette* on June 1, 1839:

> The subscriber would like to obtain the best plan of a School House two stories high — to be built of brick; the ground plan to be 45 feet square — together with a full basement and complete specifications of materials, construction and workmanship. For such an one delivered on or before June 4th to the City Clerk, I will pay five dollars. Silas Belden.

This munificent price for a design apparently produced results, for the plans of the building committee were developed that summer. The *Herald* advertised on August 6:

> Sealed proposals will be received at the office of the city clerk until Aug. 15, for building 2 school houses, one in the first and one in the second ward of the city. Payments to be made by the city as follows: $1500 on or before Dec. first, the balance in three annual payments. By order of the building committee.

Warner and Hickox, building contractors, won the commission and proceeded with construction of the first two buildings which were completed within the year.

As in the case of the Academy, the authority for the appearance these schools is Andrew Freese, who taught in one of them at the start of his career, later became the principal of the high school and superintendent of schools and wrote the first history of the schools of Cleveland. He describes these early buildings as forty-five feet and four inches square, of two stories containing four rooms, and constructed of brick. The woodcut which he published indicates that economy controlled the design, as indeed the price paid for the plan and the published cost of the buildings substantiates (Figure 32). They were simple blocks of

masonry, austerely plain in treatment and erected on a low basement. A flat string-course marked the base of the wall and a second divided the upper part into a wide band suggestive of the frieze employed in vernacular Greek Revival buildings. The two identical doors which dominated the first floor, however, were enclosed by oblong lights at top and side, a characteristic Greek Revival feature which, together with the treatment of the upper parts of the wall, were derived from a professional source. These doorways were, in fact, a simplified version of such designs as the drawing for a doorway in Edward Shaw's *Civil Architecture.* The omission of the rosette and some details in the mullions in Shaw's design was doubtless due to the need for economy.

A second group of schools became necessary in the 1850's. These were considerably larger, of three floors containing a total of five rooms, and seven of them were built at a cost of $7000 apiece. They were built after the plans of the school board, headed by Charles Bradburn and were hence known as the "Bradburn Type." These were also described and illustrated by Freese, who represents them as square blocks of brick raised on a low basement. Like the earlier type they were surmounted by a flattened hipped roof, but a few more adornments were added to the new buildings. The main entrance was divided into two doorways by three pilasters joined by a simple entablature. The facade was likewise ornamented by flat pilasters which rose through the upper floors and each had a simple capital which in turn supported a curious feature resembling a distorted S-shaped bracket. A corbel-table in low relief overlay the architrave under the projecting roof line. None of these features had a strictly orthodox character.

The Kentucky School, one of the Bradburn types though located on the west side of the river, was still standing and was photographed in 1937 (Figure 33). By that time it had

Figure 32. Prospect School, 1840.

Figure 34. Medical School, 1843-1846.

Figure 33.
Kentucky School in 1937.

undergone many changes but the main portion of the building was generally intact. A wing had been added and several new windows opened in the side wall; the main entrance had been redesigned and the corbel-table and brackets removed. But the general proportions of the building and the character of the remaining details still testified to the simple dignity of the original design.

The sober practicality of these two early designs for the schools of Cleveland which date from 1839 and 1854 was their most obvious characteristic. They were built without the advice of professional designers and with a view to the greatest possible economy. In these respects they were probably typical of a large proportion of the buildings in the city at this time.

Aside from the standard school buildings, one other more interesting structure may be considered in this category. The Medical School building erected in 1843-46 at the corner of Erie and St. Clair was a unique design (Figure 34). It was constructed of brick, wood and stone in a square block in the usual way, but the unknown designer must be credited with considerable originality for his treatment of the exterior. He chose a motif consisting of an inset panel surmounted by a simple fret and this he used as the dominant element in his design. He employed it first on an enormous scale as the corner piers of his structure between which the building seems to be suspended. This same motif on a smaller scale was again used to flank the main entrance and to mark each alternate face of the octagonal cupola which rises above the hipped roof. The second and third floors, recessed between the corner piers, were accented by four heavy but simplified classical columns. The entablature was of flat, matched boards as demanded by Greek Revival taste, its frieze penetrated by five oculi. Altogether the result was a building of some distinction but without conventional design. Unfortunately such originality became less and less common as the effects of the eclectic revivals were felt.

Aside from the handful of schools scattered through the town, the architectural character of the residential areas was determined by the quality of church and domestic buildings. By mid-century the wide streets of the best residential sections were well planted and lined with fine houses and an occasional church. Each congregation and each prosperous merchant apparently took pride in the modernity and sumptuousness of his house.

More accurate records and better photographs are available here so that the evolution of style in churches and houses may be precisely dated. The only important churches built in the 1830's clung to the traditional eastern styles. The original Old Stone Church built in 1832 and the First Baptist of 1835 were almost pure Georgian. Late in this decade the influence of the Greek Revival was felt, and at the same time the Gothic had its start. St. Mary's of 1838 was an interesting carpenter's building in which Gothic details vied with the classical forms. After 1840 the Medieval styles were almost universally used, usually Gothic, occasionally Romanesque. These styles were, to be sure, applied with an unreliable taste and varying degrees of sophistication. The first authentically Gothic church in Cleveland was Grace in 1846; the first Romanesque the Second Presbyterian in 1851. The preference for details of classical derivation which one finds in commercial and domestic building after 1840 is not shared by the churches.

The first Presbyterian Church on the Square at Ontario Street, which soon came to be known as "Old Stone," was the second house of worship to be erected in the town. It was a much more impressive building than its modest predecessor, the vernacular wooden Trinity Church of 1828. Although the Presbyterian Society was organized on September 20, 1820, it met for over a decade in various public rooms.[58] Meantime a plot of land had been purchased from Samuel Cowles on the northwest corner of Ontario at the

Figure 35. The Cleveland Grays in 1839.

Figure 36. First Baptist Church, 1834.

Figure 37. St. Mary's Church, c.1884.

Public Square and plans laid to build. The first public notice of this building appeared in the *Herald* on May 12, 1831 and it was dedicated on February 26, 1834. The *Directory* of 1837-38 provides the only detailed description:

> It is substantial edifice built of gray sand stone, rough hammered. The size of the building is 55 x 80 feet, finished in the Tuscan order of arch., with a bell section and dome. The front is divided with antaes and pilasters composed of cut stone, with a flight of spacious stone steps to its main entrance. The entablature is plain, yet tasteful and commanding. The interior is finished, on the first floor with pews, 84 in no., a full gallery, which is suspended from the ceiling by iron rods, the ceiling elliptical, the whole finish is plain but very imposing . . . .

The church appears in a painting of the Cleveland Greys on the Square executed anonymously in 1839 and now in the Western Reserve Historical Society (Figure 35).

This is a somewhat crude version of the New England meeting house. The details of capitals and moldings lack the refinement of the best 18th century work in the East but its stalwart character nonetheless is a significant change from the improvised vernacular style of Trinity.

It was completed at a time when Cleveland had momentarily attained the simple dignity of a New England village and it was consequently wholly appropriate to its setting. The use of the iron tie-rods to support the gallery on the interior, as described in the 1837-38 *Directory,* is the earliest recorded use of iron in a Cleveland building. Even at this early date a small quantity was being made in the vicinity from the ore and coal brought in by the canals. The Old Stone Church was the most impressive building in town to that date except possibly the second Court House, and was the first building to be constructed largely of cut stone. It served the community until the very end of the canal period, finally being replaced in 1853.

Of the several other churches erected at this time only one approached the solid architectural character of Old Stone. This was the First Baptist Church which was begun in 1834 on a lot at the corner of Seneca and Champlain (vacated), on the southern edge of the residential district which was just then developing (Figure 36 and Figure 10, right). The first description of the church also establishes the date of its completion: On March 2, 1836, an editorial in the *Whig* stated:

> The Baptist church, recently erected in this village, was dedicated yesterday forenoon with an appropriate and interesting ceremony. This edifice . . . is of substantial masonry, 79 ft. x 55, surmounted by a handsome spire, 150, and does great credit to the taste and liberality of the society.

McCabe's Directory of 1837-38 provides several additional details:

> It is built of brick, size 80 x 55 feet, with a spacious basement through which is the main entrance. It contains the town clock and a heavy bell — the whole crowned with a lofty spire one hundred and fifty feet high. Its order of arch. is Tuscan. The internal finish is plain but truly magnificent — finished in the Grecian Dorick [sic] order, with a full gallery suspended from the ceiling by iron Tie-rods.

This church is again a very simplified version of the older Georgian idiom despite the pride which is reflected in the description quoted above. It is likely that it would not have attracted such favorable comment in a later decade when the prosperity of the canals was making itself felt. Nonetheless it served the Baptist congregation for two decades until a new church was purchased in 1855 on Euclid and Erie Streets, a move which followed the extension of the residential district eastward on Euclid.

One other church of the 1830's is of interest, though it does not have the solid form of Old Stone and the First Baptist. This is St. Mary's, the first Catholic church in the city, which was located in the flats that it might serve the communicants from both sides of the river. Houck, the chief historian of Catholicism in Cleveland, describes it as "81 by 53 feet, having well wrought Doric columns in front, a light but substantial gallery, or organ loft, handsome ceiling, etc., and conveniently located on Columbus Street . . . ."[59] A photograph taken after a storm had blown away the pyramidal roof over the tower is the best authority for its appearance (Figure 37). Here is an interesting example of vernacular carpenter's design. The facade is Greek Revival with four fluted Doric columns supporting an entablature and pediment, and the wall behind this porch is faced with matched boards. The door and windows here are, however, ornamented by blind pointed arches and the windows in the side of the nave are also pointed. Clapboarding covers these side walls instead of the flush boards of the front. This curious admixture of classical and Gothic is continued with pointed windows and crenellations in the tower.

This church was the logical successor to the vernacular Trinity church of 1828. It was erected in the face of serious financial difficulties by a small Catholic congregation in the vicinity. No professional advice is recorded in the accounts, and none evident in the design. It is quite likely that the carpenter who was called upon to construct the building was given no more than the minimum of guidance by the building committee. A happy admixture of Greek Revival and Gothic style was the result. It was destined to be the last of the vernacular church designs in the city. The later churches abandoned, too, the classical details in favor of wholly medieval designs. The first such church was Grace, built in 1846.

Despite one recorded enlargement the old Trinity Church was outgrown by the congregations of the 1840's. To relieve the pressure of numbers the original congregation put out offshoots which met elsewhere. The first of these is recorded in the *Directory* of 1850-51 as being organized on July 9, 1845.[60] This new Episcopal group met in the Court House until Grace Church was ready for occupancy in 1848. The building committee purchased a lot on the corner of Huron

and Erie in the fall of 1846 and the cornerstone of the building was laid on September 28, 1846, but financial difficulties pursued the young society and progress was slow. By November 17, 1847, the *Whig Herald* was able to announce that "Grace Episcopal Church on the corner of Prospect and Erie Sts., is rapidly approaching completion." It was not occupied, however, until March of the following year and was even then in an incompleted state. The design was that of a professional architect identified as C. N. Otis of Buffalo, New York. It was described in the *Directory* of 1850-51 as "a brick Gothic structure 87½ x 47½, of ancient architecture, and very neat and substantial finish . . . ."

Several photographs of this church are extant. From one of these it may be seen that in contrast to the earlier "Gothic" churches of Cleveland, Trinity and St. Mary's, this building is in a mature architectural style, betraying the hand of a professional designer (Figure 38). The photograph shows that, as described, it was built of brick which appears to vary considerably in color, giving quality to the surfaces. This is a structural design of well related proportions and sheer surfaces and a consistency not elsewhere attained in the decade in Cleveland.

The elements of the design are worth noting: variation in heights of the stages of the tower and size of its openings; corner buttresses and pinnacles, lancet windows crowned by mouldings; an octagonal turret flanking the nave wall opposite the corner tower.

The lack of vernacular character in this church edifice points to a developed professional source. As has been noted, its designer was apparently a trained architect from Buffalo who was certainly familiar with the contemporary Gothic idiom. Comparison of this design with those of leading innovators of the Gothic Revival shows how such a vocabulary of Gothic forms was developed. For each element in the composition of Grace Church, a prototype may

Figure 39. St. Paul's, 1846-1856.

Figure 38. Grace Church, 1846-1847.

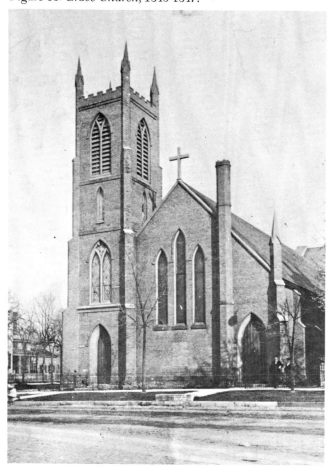

Figure 41. Second Presbyterian Church, 1851.

Figure 40. St. Paul's interior.

be found in the work of such men as Richard Upjohn and the firm of Town and Davis. The four-staged, square, corner tower and the overall arrangement of the facade with its triple lancet window and octagonal turret are found in Grace Church, Providence, by Upjohn. The proportions of the tower and the design of such details as the pinnacles at its corners are related to Christ Church, Brooklyn, by the same architect. The corner buttresses set at an angle, on the other hand, are seldom used by Upjohn but are a characteristic feature of Davis' designs as in the project for Grace Church, Broadway. Lancet windows crowned by mouldings above the spring-line, and attached buttresses with a series of setbacks are common to many designs by these eastern architects. In the hands of these leading practitioners such elements of Gothic design became a collection of terms, a vocabulary of design, which could then be used in endless variations as need arose. An idiom was thus developed which permitted the dissemination of a variegated but homogeneous Gothic style across the country in the early years of the Gothic Revival. Grace Church in Cleveland is a case in point.

The most sophisticated Gothic design among Cleveland churches of the canal period was St. Pauls' (Figure 39). This congregation, like that of Grace Church, separated from overcrowded Trinity in 1846 and employed the city's leading architectural firm of Heard and Porter to design its new building. It was commenced in 1848 on Euclid Avenue, by that time a fashionable residential street, but not completed for a decade due to a disastrous fire. In exterior appearance St. Pauls' is quite clearly directly dependent upon the design of Trinity on Broadway, New York, by Richard Upjohn. The distinctive tower of four stages with pinnacles and octagonal spire are unmistakable, and the row of pinnacles sprouting from the attached buttresses which mark the side walls are very like those of Trinity. Only on the interior is a major difference found (Figure 40). Upjohn's church has three aisles, covered by ribbed vaults, whereas the Cleveland version by Heard and Porter consists of a single nave roofed in wood. Thus Heard and Porter obviously lifted the design from Upjohn but so interpreted it as to reduce the structural problems to a scale which they could handle, a performance entirely characteristic of the time.

The same basic form of building is found in the last two important churches of the canal period, but in these the detail is Romanesque, or Norman as it was then called, rather than Gothic. Second Presbyterian was built near the Square on Superior by the same firm Heard and Porter (Figure 41). The description in the *Directory* of 1853 is interesting:[61]

> The front is of brown sandstone, with side and rear walls of brick, 124 feet long by 70 wide, with steeple and spire 195 feet high. The interior walls are elegantly finished with fresco painting. The basement is arranged with lecture room, 62 by 58 feet; a ladies society room and session room, each 27 by 31 feet, and 11 feet high, all of which are connected by folding doors, making a hall that will conveniently seat about one thousand persons. The audience room on the main floor is 63 by 98 feet, and 39 feet high, with gallery 10 feet deep, extending on three sides of the room. There are 174 slips on the principal floor, and 32 in the gallery, furnishing about 1200 sittings. The building is in the Norman style of architecture, in a modified form; and in architectural beauty, and elegant finish, is not excelled by any building in our city. The design is by Messrs. Heard and Porter, under whose superintendence the building was erected.

The chapel which projects from the side of the building was added, according to Pomeroy, in 1870. On October 9, 1876, this church was gutted by fire, and had to be removed. It is indicative of the direction of Cleveland's subsequent development that the congregation chose a site far to the

Figure 42. Plymouth Church, 1853.

east at Prospect and Sterling (East 30th) on which to build in the following years.

The *Directory's* description of the Second Presbyterian Church as being "in the Norman style of architecture, in a modified form" is not entirely inapt. This is the first major church in Cleveland to make use of Romanesque detail. Its octagonal tower and slender turrets were decorated by crenellations but the gable ends and the main stage of the tower as well as the turrets had corbel tables and all the openings were round-headed. The flexibility of the basement rooms reflects the initiative of Charles W. Heard's designs. Despite the Romanesque detail this design retains something of the vernacular character in the unconventional shape of the tower and the use of octagonal turrets as buttresses at the corners. It is just such free use of forms which gives to the work of this firm its unhackneyed character at this time.

The last important church to be completed prior to the union of Cleveland and Ohio City in 1854 was Plymouth. This congregation was detached from Old Stone, and erected its church on Euclid and Erie Streets. The cornerstone was dedicated on May 29, 1852, and its completion was noticed in flattering terms by the *Daily True Democrat* on July 13, 1853: "The Plymouth Church of Cleveland was dedicated last week. It is a beautiful structure, massive yet elegant, large but harmonious both in its proportions and ornaments. It will accommodate 1200 people and is fitted up so that the speaker's voice will be heard in the remotest parts of the auditorium."

A photograph of Plymouth Church, taken in 1870 before extensive remodelling had changed its character in 1879-80, shows that it had much the same overall character as its immediate predecessors (Figure 42). Like St. Pauls' and the Second Presbyterian it had a single nave dominated by a particularly massive central tower and spire. A triple entrance, in this case, admitted to the body of the church. The walls were plain which gave the building a heavy and severe appearance but the details of ornament were sharp and professional in character. All the openings were round-headed, and the gable, the side walls and bell-stage of the tower carried heavy corbel-tables. Already in this design there is something of the bulkiness and unwieldy character which was soon to become so typical of Victorian design in the next decades.

This handful of churches in Cleveland, erected in the twenty-odd year period of the canal era, reveal many things about the development of the town. Changes of location, from the northwest quadrant to the Public Square and then farther and farther east, are an index to the migration of the residential district. Changes in style, from the Georgian through the Greek Revival to the Gothic and Romanesque reflect the shifting fashions of the time. Changes in materials, from wood to brick and then to cut stone; and of skills, from the simple vernacular to sophisticated professionalism mark the evolution of the architectural profession in this period. It is by these processes that the cities of the United States acquired their architectural character in the 19th century.

As in the case of commercial architecture in the canal period, so also with private residences the large majority were inexpensively built by artisans and made no pretensions to architectural style. For all this there was a growing number of fine houses in town in the canal period as prosperity increased and as better materials and skills became available. By mid-century, as has been seen, the most fashionable streets were flanked by solidly-built homes, often of brick or cut stone and designed in the latest fashion. In the early 1830's Georgian remnants were still to be found, as in the Crittenden house, but in 1836 the Erastus Gaylord house was predominantly Greek Revival with a large portico rising through two floors. This classical fashion was very persistent, lasting throughout the period and in fact reaching its most pretentious stage in the Worthington residence of 1852. It had rivals, however, as early as the 1840's, chiefly the Gothic. This style was to be found in a vernacular version in the Bolton house of 1846 and in a heavy stone interpretation in the famous home of H. B. Payne in 1849. Near mid-century Italian forms became popular, especially those published by A. J. Downing in his *Cottage Residences*. These styles were found in Cleveland in the Henry B. Gaylord house of 1849, and the two Perkins houses of 1851-55, among many others.

This evolution starts with the Crittenden house which was completed in 1833 on the Public Square at Ontario Street opposite the First Presbyterian Church (Figure 43). At this time the Square was becoming the fashionable residential district of town and Crittenden, as one of its leading merchants, erected the most ambitious home yet undertaken. It was built of brick with wood trim painted white and with green shutters. It was largely a Georgian design, with the five-bay facade and central door, four chimneys and balustrade above the roof line, although the pitch of the roof and the recessed doorway indicate the beginnings of Greek Revival taste. This was a conservative building of a style which was still being used in many parts of New England, and its appropriateness to the village character of Cleveland in the 1830's is suggested by the painting of the Cleveland Grays in 1839 where it appears to the right of Old Stone Church (Figure 35).

A second house of this same period comes closer to the Greek Revival taste. In 1832 that same Levi Johnson who was the pioneer builder of the early days erected a home for Richard Winslow on the southeast corner of the Square (Figure 44). The facade is much the same as that of the Crittenden house, but the details are Greek Revival. All walls are smooth-finished and the roof is so flattened as to

Figure 43. Crittenden House in 1874.

Figure 44. Winslow House, 1832.

Figure 45. Erastus Gaylord House, 1836.

Figure 46. Anson Smith House, 1846.

be completely hidden by the solid balustrade above the cornice, giving the facade a strong horizontal emphasis. The entablature is classical rather than Georgian in proportions and the central doorway is covered by a portico supported on Doric columns. The house is neither traditional nor entirely Greek Revival, but an admixture of both.

The Greek Revival soon thereafter became the dominant style and the Georgian had disappeared by the later 1830's. A characteristic residence was the home of Erastus Gaylord built in 1836 (Figure 45). This was situated on Kinsman Street where a new residential district of these years was rapidly developing. It was a stone house, in itself a sign of sophistication, and had a two-story central pavilion and single story wings which was a popular arrangement in the Greek Revival style. A monumental Greek portico dominated the facade and a full entablature encircled the entire central pavilion. This home is an early example of the monumental effects, executed in durable materials, which marked the beginnings of a highly prosperous period in the life of the town.

The logical successor to this experiment with the large scale portico was the still purer Greek Revival home of Anson Smith in 1846 (Figure 46). In the Schultze drawing of Euclid Avenue in 1846-47, this house was the largest and most imposing. A photograph of a later date shows that it was placed well back from the street with a spacious yard on the sides. It was of two stories, built of brick and raised on a low basement. The dominant feature was, of course, the wooden Doric portico of four monumental columns and a full entablature which encompasses the entire house. The doorway beneath the portico is also marked by pilasters and a full entablature. The temple form without lateral wings was here used for the first time in Cleveland. The multiplication of such well situated and handsomely designed houses was responsible for the fame which Euclid Avenue attained in these, and especially in later, years as one of the most beautiful residential streets in the country.

The Greek Revival ran its course in the period of the canals in Cleveland. One of the last and most elaborate of the residences in this style was that of George Worthington, built in 1852 on Euclid Avenue at Forest Street (East 37th) (Figure 47). When built it lay well beyond the crowded center of town at the very outskirts of the residential district, and was the forerunner of a row of pretentious residences which lined his part of Euclid Avenue in the 1860's and 1870's. Following the example of the Worthington house these were set farther from the street than the earlier homes to take advantage of the ridge which lies just north of Euclid. The generous pattern of this district evoked widespread enthusiasm. It was fully developed by 1876 when it was thus described by William Payne in his volume, *Cleveland Illustrated*:

> Other world-famous streets may have grander architecture for a short distance; single lawns may be more lavishly decorated with flowerbeds and statuary; or there may be other isolated beauties which surpass anything this famous avenue can show. But no avenue in the world can present to the delighted visitor such a continuous succession of charming residences and such uniformly beautiful grounds for so great a distance. . . . . Each house has grounds more or less spacious, stretching from the ridge on which the house stands down to the line of the street at some distance; the turf of these lawns is almost invariably of velvety softness and of a rich green, showing watchful care and liberal expenditure in its maintenance.

The Worthington house itself was of brick, built on a stone basement. Both the main pavilion and the lower wings were ornamented by an elaborate Ionic order in wood surmounted by a heavy balustrade. These were beautifully wrought and handsomely proportioned orders which vouched

Figure 47. George Worthington House, 1852.

for the high quality of taste and workmanship which had been attained by this time. The plates of Asher Benjamin or Minard Lafever were available as models for such a portico. One of the features of this late Greek Revival house which was symptomatic of the change in taste at the end of the canal period is the height of the windows. These reflect the higher ceilings on the interior, comparable to those found in the Weddell House and in Northrop and Spangler's Block. They indicate the beginning of a tendency toward greater interior spaciousness which was to culminate in the buildings of the next two decades.

Meantime during the 1840's the Gothic style was introduced to compete with the Greek for fashionable honors. The publications of Downing, William Brown and Edward Shaw among others popularized the style and the practice of leading architects, Richard Upjohn in particular, gave it authority. One of the earliest houses to adopt the new fashion was the house of Thomas Bolton in 1846 (Figure 48). It was a small cottage with lateral one-story wings and a low spreading gable in the Greek tradition, but the ornamental details were new. The barge-board under the gable roof was elaborately carved in a series of slender arches resembling a decorative corbel table, and the single window in this gable was a double lancet under a pointed enframing arch. All three porches on the facade were decorated with Tudor arches in wood and crowned by crenellations. These fashionable Gothic details had been added to a simple Greek Revival building in response to the changing fashions of the time. The sources may well have been Downing. In his 1842 edition, for example, the details of a porch closely resembles that of the Bolton house.

Of the many Gothic Revival houses of these years in Cleveland one of the finest and fortunately one of the most completely documented is that of Henry B. Payne, built in 1849 on Euclid at Perry Street (Figure 49). It attracted the attention of the *Daily True Democrat* on March 10, 1849:

> Among the finest houses put up in this city for the last few years, we think the house of H. B. Payne, Esq., on the corner of Euclid and Perry Streets, is the best. Its outer proportions and appearance are admirable; its style of architecture massive and enduring — its finish beautiful, and all interior arrangements, for elegance, comfort, convenience and health, equal to any residence we have ever seen. This house is well worth looking at by those who intend to build fine houses here this season; and there are a number . . . .
> Mr. C. W. Heard is the architect of the house of Mr. Payne.

Unlike the vernacular Bolton house, this was a pretentious mansion of cut stone in the most fashionable Gothic manner. It lacks the picturesque silhouette and irregular plan often found in this style, but all of the authentic Gothic details are there. The steep-pitch of roof with carved barge boards, the wooden pinnacle and paired chimneys, the pointed windows and projecting bays on brackets: these constitute the vocabulary of the Gothic Revival. Upjohn and A. J. Davis had been building such residences in the east since the mid-thirties, and the details of ornament were available in the carpenters' manuals of Downing, Edward Shaw or William Brown.

As elsewhere, the Gothic style was of short duration in Cleveland. It was expensive and difficult to build because of the variety of forms called for, and it was as well too exotic and arbitrary for the average taste. Perhaps for these reasons it was very conservatively used in Cleveland and by 1850 was already out of favor. As it was abandoned, its place was quickly taken by the more practical forms of the Italian manner.

This style was considered at the time to be peculiarly American, and in fact was often called the "Tuscan or American Style." It became popular in the decade preceding the

Figure 48. Thomas Bolton House, 1846.

Civil War; thereafter it was replaced by the ubiquitous Mansard roof. Even more clearly than its predecessors, this Italian manner consisted of a vocabulary of useful forms which could be freely and readily adapted to a variety of problems, making it the most flexible style yet devised in American architecture. These houses were usually built of brick or stone with sheer wall surfaces and cubic forms. Flattened hipped roofs with overhanging eaves supported by brackets were common, and openings were round-headed. Stone balconies, open or hooded with a metal canopy were frequently used. The plans varied considerably, some being extensions of the compact Greek Revival types, but many were freely disposed, providing a greater variety of plan.

This style seems to have been developed by Richard Up-john. In any case it appears in its mature form in his King House in Newport in 1845-46. This design was published by Downing in 1853 which, of course, assured its popularity. In Cleveland, variants upon the style dominated the fashionable residential districts in the 1850's.

Chronologically the first of the fine residences in this style was the home of Henry B. Gaylord on Euclid. It may be seen situated fourth from the right in the photograph of that street (Figure 20). A closer view of this house shows that it was built of brick with stone and wood trim (Figure 50). The main block was of two stories and surmounted by a flattened hipped roof. The heavy cornice was supported by thick brackets grouped in pairs which gave a massive character to the whole design. The single wing at the west side of the main block had a similar cornice above solid columns and the doorway was recessed behind an entablature decorated with classical revival motives. This was an expensive and well designed residence, massively proportioned and solidly constructed.

Figure 49. Henry B. Payne House, 1849.

Figure 50. Henry B. Gaylord House, 1849.

In the same view of Euclid Avenue the two houses on the right hand side of the photograph (Figure 20) are early examples of a cubic house form covered by a hipped roof with widespread eaves supported by brackets which became very popular in this decade. The characteristic feature of a curved moulding over the windows and doors carried on small brackets, was applied to many building types in the late 1850's, including schools and business buildings as well as residences.

These two houses were conservative in plan, retaining the compact form which had been popular for several decades. But in the same years the fully developed Italian Villa style was brought directly to Cleveland by one of the leading architects in the country. In 1851-53 Richard Upjohn designed a house for Joseph Perkins which was built on Euclid Avenue[62] (Figure 51). The flexibility of the Italian style is fully exploited in Upjohn's many houses in this style in the early 1850's. In the Perkins house the projecting pavilions indicate flexible interior spaces which was the chief advantage of this style. By reason of the simple cubic forms variety was possible without the structural difficulties of the Gothic and it was much cheaper to build. It was quickly taken up by local designers as in the neighboring Jacob Perkins house, where another combination of the accepted forms was worked out (Figure 52). These Italian villas bring the canal period to a close as far as residential design is concerned.

In the transformation of Cleveland which took place between 1830 and 1854 the foundations of the modern city were laid. The forms which subsequently arose on these foundations were varied and complex, and adapted to the demands of industrialization and to the still greater complexities of recent times. But for all these later changes the legacy of this second quarter of the century continued to control the form of the city. This legacy was twofold: it was

physical in the total form of the town of 1854; it was as well methodological in the usages and procedures which had developed during this quarter century. The precedents then established effected the future course of development just as irrevocably as did the physical objects on the ground.

It is true, of course, that the mercantile town inherited certain accomplished facts from the earlier period which severely channeled its progress. As has been seen, the original plan was not entirely adapted to the terrain and was rigidly mechanical in character, both of which deficiencies placed the subsequent period under a severe handicap. The twin forces of tradition and real estate speculation played their decisive roles here. Again, the business center on Superior Street had already by 1830 developed a pattern of overcrowding as Whelpley's prints of a year or so later suggest. Finally, the tendency to a varied character in architectural forms was standard procedure by the end of the first quarter of the century. These were elements in the town's character for which the canal era cannot be held responsible.

But these deficiencies were scarcely noticeable in the New England village which the original planners had envisaged. The Whelpley prints of 1833 reveal an open, balanced town which doubtless functioned very well within the demands made upon it. The situation became awkward only as it became complicated by the pressures of expansion. It was at this point, after 1830, that control and direction were most needed. The canal period was the time when the destiny of the city, as a city, was decided.

The decisions made and the physical facts accumulated between 1830 and 1854 were many and their effects, both for good and for ill, were lasting. In the expansion of the plan of the town certain of the measures adopted were wise. The subdivision of the central area by streets on the gridiron

Figure 51. Joseph Perkins House, 1851-1853.

plan was for the most part adequately controlled in order to avoid too great a multiplication of narrow ways. Beyond the center to east and south the design of wide radiating avenues, encouraged by the original survey of the ten-acre lots, provided arteries which converged on the civic and mercantile center of town. These wide thoroughfares were quite adequate until, within the twentieth century, the problems of mass transportation overwhelmed the whole central area.

In the newer sections of town to the east and south of the center, however, serious mistakes were made. As the town expanded the street pattern was extended in a perfectly mechanical fashion. Based upon the precedent set by the original plan, the new streets defined regular oblongs between the radiating ways and were lined by narrow lots. Thus the rigidity of the village design was clamped upon the growing city despite the apparent flexibility of the diverging thoroughfares. At the same time, and as part of this process, the economic pressures of the times had their effect. Land speculation, which was a condition of the original design and purpose of the town, became an increasingly potent force in its expansion and was less and less adequately controlled as profits became easier and more tempting.

Meantime in adapting itself to the civic responsibilities thrust upon it by the expansion of town the council experienced both success and failure. The absolute necessities of water supply and lighting were provided with commendable energy. But when mere convenience was to be served, dilatory tactics or downright failure marked their policy. The streets and sidewalks were improved slowly and only after repeated and often ill-tempered urging by the citizens, and the provision of public grounds was never achieved at all despite constant demand for a more far-seeing policy.

In the matter of controlling the architectural growth of

Figure 52. Jacob Perkins House, 1853.

the city, the canal period was marked by few successes and many failures. The sole instance of a sensible zoning regulation was the prohibition against wooden structures in order to curb the disastrous fires in the business district. In all other respects the various areas of town developed without any guidance, with no regard for either the public interest or for the preservation of established values. The results were unfortunate. In the preponderantly wholesale area along the banks of the river the most conspicuous result was deterioration, produced by a multiplication of warehouses and stock piles. A mercantile slum was already being formed in this area and meantime the allocation of waterfront sites to public use was entirely neglected. In the highly industrialized era to come the precedents thus set were to prove ultimately destructive of whole areas of town. In the retail sections most of the older wooden buildings were replaced with brick structures and an occasional fine building of cut stone. Again, however, no overall design directed this growth, with the result that the retail areas became crowded and competitive in architectural character. The streets became lined solidly to the sidewalks with little regard for reasonable order and space in the area as a whole. Moreover, the lateral extension of these concerns resulted in the wholesale destruction of neighboring residential units. The displaced homes and their accompanying churches and schools moved eastward and southeast where new residential areas, some of considerable dignity, arose. These avenues were, in the best examples, well designed, the houses well placed in relation to the street and generously spaced. These became the most attractive parts of the town and in them the ambitions of the prosperous classes found their outlet.

From the vantage point of the present, now that the destructive effects of these methods have been demonstrated, it is difficult to justify the short-sightedness of the policies of these decades. The reasoning of the time, however, is clear. The period was one of expansion and mounting prosperity based on commerce. The town was rapidly emerging from a primitive state. All encouragement was hence given to progress. Each new building erected or new enterprise undertaken, every increment in population or new street added was enthusiastically noted. The preoccupation with immediate returns and the eagerness for expansion completely obscured the vision of the future effects of these policies. As in the extension of the town plan, so in the architectural growth which arose on that plan expediency was allowed full sway. There is no evidence that serious thought was at any time given to long-range plans for the town as a whole. The age of city planning had not yet arrived.

Finally, the canal period was marked by several important trends in the character of individual buildings in Cleveland. Inspired by the changing fashions presented by the handbooks and by the practice of leading innovators, the designers of Cleveland lined their streets with a sequence of styles. Barely was one form accepted when it was replaced by a new taste. Heterogeneity could be the only result. This situation was far from being unique. The same pattern was common to all parts of the country, particularly in the rapidly growing commercial centers. Cleveland became in this respect a typical community of the United States during the canal period.

Nonetheless, architectural design had unquestionably progressed since the village stage. The use of finer materials, aided by a number of improvements in technical methods, produced a better quality of building. The skills of the designer increased proportionately. In the best examples of each building type a rising standard of excellence was evident. The sophistication, however, severely effected indigenous design. The number of buildings in a vernacular idiom declined as the taste for "official" styles spread. This is the beginning of a tendency which ultimately destroyed the originality of the craftsman which had made such important contributions to American art.

By and large it must be concluded that the overall development of the town of Cleveland was not a healthy one during the crucial period of its rapid expansion between 1830 and the industrial age. Too many physical obstacles to continued sound development were erected; too many dangerous precedents on which subsequent periods were to build were then established. These augured ill for the fortunes of the industrial city and the modern metropolis. Their aftermath becomes painfully clear in the events of succeeding decades.

CHAPTER FOUR

THE INDUSTRIAL CITY 1854-1875

In the third quarter of the century Cleveland entered a second period of rapid expansion and pervading change. In the two previous decades water-borne transportation had been the chief stimulus to growth. Now after mid-century the impetus was provided by industry and the railroads, and for the second time the town was transformed. A new wave of immigration was fostered and the city limits were extended, first by the inclusion of Ohio City and then by the addition of large areas to the east and south. The original town center became congested and a network of new streets was laid out and quickly occupied on the edges of town. With lateral expansion better transportation was needed, requiring street improvement and systems of public transportation. Water supply and street lighting were extended to new areas, and for the first time municipal systems of refuse collection and sewerage were undertaken. Grave issues, unprecedented in simpler times, had now to be faced, in particular those of air and water pollution which were by-products of industrialization. As the population increased and the town spread out, the need for parks became a serious issue.

Some of these problems which accompanied industrialization were without precedent and had to be solved by improvisation. Many, however, began in the canal period and were merely aggravated by industrialization. By 1854,

for example, the street pattern in the center of town was already fixed and large areas were built over. In consequence the period of industrialization could make few constructive changes even had it so desired. To the contrary, the established character of each part of town became more deeply imprinted under the new pressures. The mercantile crowding in the flats on each side of the river was increased as industry and the railroads moved into this area. The retail districts were still more densely planted with stores and offices, and gaps in the residential streets were closed.

Under these conditions many difficulties arose and new procedures to cope with them would have been salutary. None was forthcoming. The precedents set in the canal period were as binding as the physical forms on the ground. Economic prosperity was still the prime mover and its own justification. Expediency rather than planning continued to guide development. Real estate speculation took an even greater toll. But now the effects of these methods became far more serious. In the canal period they produced some inconvenience. Under industrialization they resulted in malfunction and disease in the body of the city.

The new era was introduced soon after the mid-century mark was passed. The most important single event of this time was the extension to Cleveland of the railroads.[63] The first attempts to develop railroads in Ohio date as far back as 1836, but it was not until 1851 that a route finally entered the city itself. This was the Cleveland, Columbus and Cincinnati from the south, which laid its tracks in the flats. It was soon followed by two more roads which came in from the east, the Cleveland and Pittsburgh in 1852 and the Cleveland and Erie soon thereafter. By 1857 Cleveland was connected with Youngstown and hence assured a constant supply of coal to feed its growing iron manufacturers. Due to the level terrain of large parts of Ohio and due as well to the prevalence of gravel for ballast, timber for ties, and an iron industry to supply rails and rolling stock, the railroads flourished in the late 1850's in Ohio. By 1861 she led the nation in miles of railroads in active service. Cleveland soon became the terminus of lines from the south and an important way station on the level lakeshore route to the west. First as a supplement and then as an unwelcome competitor to the canals, the railroads increased the passenger and freight traffic to Cleveland many-fold in the next decades. They provided a vital link in the transportation facilities essential to the development of the city as an industrial center.

Transportation by water remained important. The strategic location of Cleveland was at no time better demonstrated than in this period when lake traffic played so vital a role in the expansion of industry. The heavy freight boats which multiplied on the lake provided an inexpensive means of transporting bulk loads, especially the hematite ores of the Superior region which stimulated and maintained the iron industry in Ohio. Even the canals, though now in decreasing volume due to the competition of the rails, continued to supply the city from the south.

To accommodate these carriers terminal facilities had to be further developed. New piers were constructed on the lake front adjacent to the river mouth in 1853 to provide convenient dockage for the freighters and equally for the railroads which converged on this point. Warehouses and depots were built on these piers and increased in number along the banks of the river itself, where new wharfs were required to accommodate the industries moving into the flats. Bridges were needed to link the recently united towns on either side of the stream and to carry the east-west railroad lines. These seriously interfered with the growing harbor traffic and many complaints were registered that Cleveland was losing trade because of the inadequacy of her harbor.

After 1854 efforts were redoubled to provide a deeper and wider channel. At great expense which mounted yearly the ship channel was deepened first near the river mouth and in later years in the upper river as activity on the flats moved inland. With the constant increase in the size of the lake freighters a wider as well as a deeper channel was required, especially at the sharp turns in the river's winding course. The problem was a continuing one, becoming more and more acute with the multiplication of industry.

As a terminus for both railroad and water transportation, Cleveland was in an ideal position in the late 1850's to attract the industries which depended on an abundance of raw materials. Promptly with the arrival of the railroads Cleveland began to change its character from that of a mercantile town to the industrial city it has now become. The number and size of its factories increased yearly in the next few decades. At the head of the list was the processing of iron ore and the manufacture of iron and steel products. These were the key industries, the largest in scale and number of plants and the ones most influential on the character of the town.

The manufacture of iron products was not totally new to Cleveland. As early as 1834 the Cuyahoga Steam Furnace Company was incorporated to manufacture cast and

Figure 53. Plan of Cleveland, 1861.

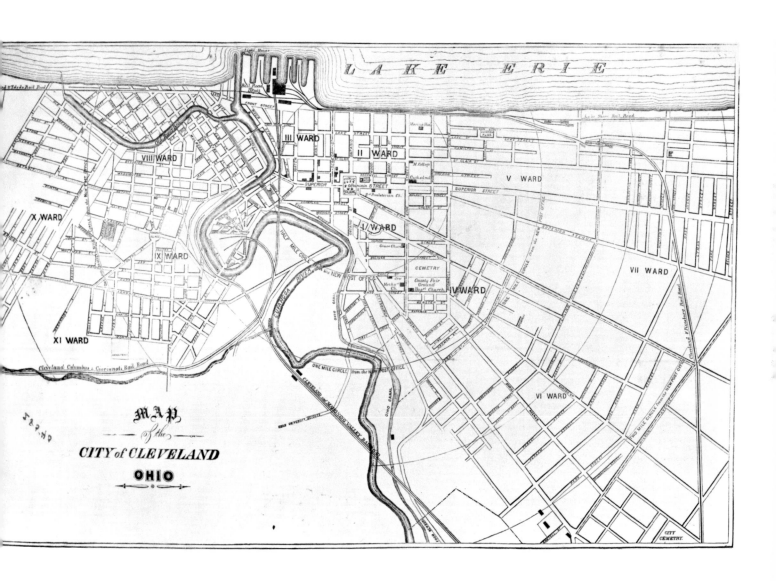

MAP
of the
CITY of CLEVELAND
OHIO

wrought iron as well as the boilers and engines from which its name was derived. The *Directory* of 1837 listed four iron foundries and steam engine "manufactories" in the city. By 1846 this number had increased to six and a steady addition to this figure was made in the subsequent years. These were, however, small works capable of producing limited quantities of iron products at best. They were dependent upon the low-grade ores of Ohio, and upon the slow transportation of the canals for both iron and coal supplies. The railroads multiplied the receipts of coal, particularly after 1857 when Youngstown was directly connected to Cleveland by rail. Then in 1856 the first Superior hematite, a high grade ore soon to become available in large quantities, reached the city.

The interest and activity caused by the development of the iron industry is amply reflected in the newspapers of this decade. Repeated reference is made to new mills, the value of investments in these enterprises, and the quantity of iron produced. Advancement of the technology of the industry was rapid and the processing plants spread along the river and the railroad right-of-way where adequate supplies of ore and coal and transport for their finished products were all assured.

The combined stimulation of transportation and industry in the city of Cleveland effected its character in many ways. It assumed even more than hitherto the character of a "boom" town. The first symptom was, of course, another upswing in the population. Shortly after the Civil War the population had increased nearly four-fold since the advent of the railroads, and in the decade after 1860 alone had more than doubled. It stood at almost 93,000 in 1870.[64]

Despite this volume of immigration the city limits of 1854 provided sufficient space for the new residents for some years. Except at the center of town the lots were but thinly populated and were therefore capable of absorbing most of the increase. In 1867, however, two large segments of the south were added (Figures 6, H & I), and in 1872 East Cleveland was incorporated with Cleveland (Figure 6 L). Meantime within the city as defined in 1854 many new streets had been laid out. The map of the 1861-2 *Directory* shows the changes made in the late 1850's (Figure 53). At the center of the town virtually no additions to the street pattern had been made since mid-century. This area had already become so densely built up that new streets could have been cut through only at exorbitant cost. It was less expensive to expand laterally and the additions to be seen in this plan of 1861 are hence found on the outskirts of town. By the date of this map two concentrations of new streets had been laid down to the east of Sterling Avenue (East 30th), one to the north of Superior Avenue and a second south of Cedar Street. In each the pattern of the ten-acre lots, laid down in 1797, controlled the design. But it is interesting to note that the blocks north of Euclid Avenue were not divided by new streets, although they were now the site of a row of expensive residences. Payne's Pasture of earlier fame, now owned by the town's richest men, was still persistently maintaining itself in the face of the pressures of expansion.

Ultimately the area within the city limits was built up sufficiently to warrant additional developments beyond the borders of the town. By the end of the 1860's, in fact, the boundaries of 1854 could no longer contain the swelling population. The street map in the *Directory* of 1868 shows a new pattern of streets to the east of Willson Avenue (Figure 54). These were the first to be laid out beyond the ten-acre lots, the east boundary of which was Willson Avenue itself. Hence the new plots and the street pattern on which they were shaped were no longer controlled by the survey lines of these out-lots as laid down in 1797. For

Figure 54. Plan of Cleveland, 1868.

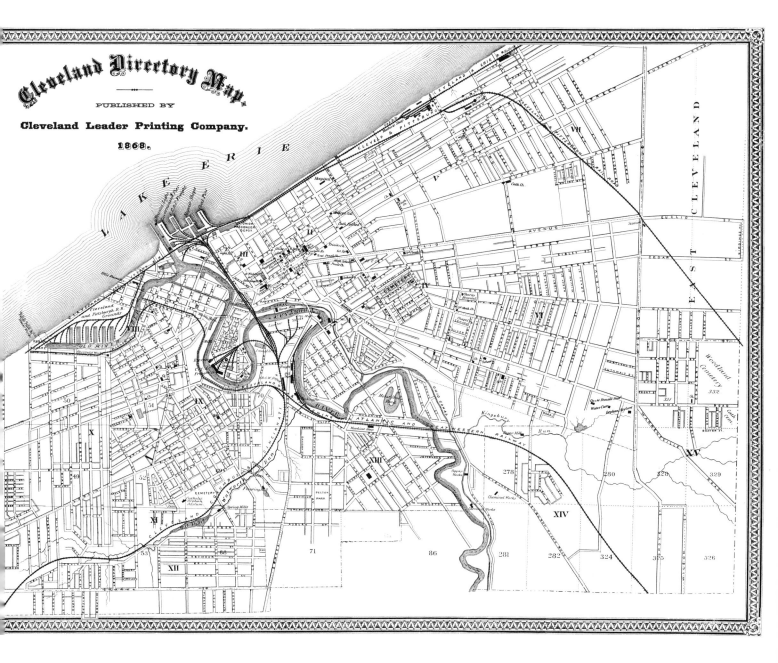

Cleveland Directory Map.

PUBLISHED BY

Cleveland Leader Printing Company.

1868.

the first time the city had outgrown the limits marked out by the original surveyors and it may be seen that the pattern of cross streets between radiating avenues was immediately abandoned. The pattern now returned to the simpler if more mechanical gridiron plan.

During this expansion the new forces of the period wrought many changes within the city itself. In effecting these changes the railroads played a decisive role. In a sense they were the central factor in the formation of industrial Cleveland, and unfortunately they were potentially a destructive force. The benefits which they introduced were many, but the carving out of rights-of-way involved numerous cuts and fills which disrupted the natural terrain and intersected the traffic arteries of the city; the terminals, yards and repair facilities and the steam engines themselves produced cinders and smoke which blanketed the areas adjacent to the tracks. In addition, the railroads brought with them a string of dependent factories which multiplied the problems.

Under the conditions which brought the railroads to Cleveland no adequate control of these problems was possible. In the 1850's railroad development was in a chaotic state, involving dozens of competing, independent companies each with its own facilities. Enthusiasm for the new systems was widespread and they received generous support. With an eye to the expected benefits, the state and local governments gave the companies every encouragement. The state legislature granted liberal charters and voted public money to their aid. The city of Cleveland itself pledged its credit to a number of companies and permitted them all possible freedom in the location of rights-of-way and terminal and repair facilities. These circumstances did not conduce to adequate direction and control and the city could not anticipate the destructive effects of the railroads on the city itself since they had no precedent to guide them. The lines were laid on the most convenient terrain, according to expediency, and the sheds, terminals and yards followed.

In specific cases the results of these policies were unwholesome. The site chosen for the Cleveland and Erie was seriously so. It was laid out on the level terrain along the shore of the lake and by thus pre-empting the shore line made impossible the development of the entire lake front within the city for recreation and residential use. Moreover this line and the Cleveland and Pittsburgh established yards and service buildings just east of the old Clinton Park development which had been established in 1835 as a protected residential community. By 1850 this was one of the better districts of town for homes. It had a fine site near the lake and was well removed from the crowded center of town. The location of these railroad facilities next door destroyed these values and as a result the subsequent history of this district was one of deterioration and decline.

The Cleveland and Pittsburgh line cut diagonally across the city in a southeasterly course, crossing Willson Avenue at Euclid. Thus the most fashionable street in town which was at that moment pushing its row of fine homes eastward was interrupted by the debris and smoke-producing railroad. Though Euclid Avenue succeeded in maintaining its integrity for several decades, the seeds of decay were planted as soon as the railroad arrived.

The railroads themselves were the cause of much deterioration, but their destructive force did not, unfortunately, stop there. The industries which they stimulated and encouraged naturally chose their sites near the right-of-way. Only there, or near the water, could they be assured of the transportation upon which they depended. As early as 1854 the *Forest City Democrat* announced the establishment of two iron works beside the railway along the lake front. Three years later the King Wrought Iron Bridge Works was located near Hamilton Street on the same line and the Cleveland Tube Works arose in the same vicinity in the

Figure 55. King Wrought Iron Bridge Company in 1876.

Figure 57. Glidden & Joy Varnish Company, c. 1882.

Figure 56.
Younglove Company in 1876.

next decade (Figure 55). All these plants required sidings, material dumps and service sheds which were placed adjacent to residential areas. Thus was fostered an abrupt change in the character of the lake front district which produced disintegration.

A manufacturing plant arose in 1870 a short distance from Euclid Avenue at Willson on this same railroad line. This was the Younglove Company, a forerunner of many more which were to be strung out along the route of this rail line through the heart of one of the residential districts of town (Figure 56). The Glidden and Joy Varnish Company was established in 1875 at the crossing of the same railroad and the New York, Chicago and St. Louis, dissecting the residential district east of Woodland Cemetery and producing a nuisance of odor as well as smoke in the neighborhood (Figure 57). The process was cumulative and by 1876 Payne could describe the routes of the three principal roads as entering Cleveland past a "succession of iron mills, foundaries [sic] and manufactures . . . numerous wire and steel works" and "numerous and extensive oil refineries." The fruits of the permissive policy which gave the railroads access to all parts of town were now in evidence.

Though swathes of deterioration were thus cut through the town, largely by the railroads, the flats remained the center of industrial and wholesale development. Here the main terminal facilities of both water and land transportation converged, encouraging further concentrations of depots and warehouses on the one hand and the development of industrial plants on the other. Congestion mounted and the confusion already established before industrialization was greatly aggravated. To the already existing stock piles and warehouses of the mercantile firms were now added the material dumps, slag heaps and debris of the new factories. Within a short distance from the civic center

of town an industrial slum was formed, and this disorder spread upstream to the south as the river was deepened and widened to admit larger ships. Terminal facilities and shops for the railroads were located here and the narrower valleys of the side streams, Kingsbury Run to the east and Walworth Run on the west, were invaded, thus driving wedges of industry into the town on each side of the river. The entire area of the flats was ultimately taken over and the character of this part of central Cleveland was established and persists to the present day. A bird's-eye view of the river valley in 1878 reveals the density of these concentrations of warehouses, plants and railroad facilities covering the banks of the river and the entire area of Cleveland Centre, and even stretching into the distance to the south (Figure 58).

In addition to producing disintegration on the flats this industrial concentration along the edges of the river had a further indirect result. The merchant firms continued to grow in proportion to the increase in population and the improvement in facilities for trade. With the competition of industry they could no longer find room to expand in the flats and were in many cases forced out of the valley into the town itself. The retail district off Superior Street which was still in the process of wiping out the original residential district of town along Water and Bank Streets was once more transformed. Since it was the location most convenient to docks and terminals, the warehouses and depots of the wholesale trade filtered into this area. Thus the transformation of the first residential community in town was finally completed. This area may be seen in the background of a view of the northwest quadrant of the city taken from the roof of the Forest City House about 1880 (Figure 59).

The growing population of Cleveland called into being a proportionate increase in retail trade. Many new stores

Figure 58. Bird's-eye view of the Flats in 1878.

VIEW OF PIVOT SPAN

FROM THE EAST SIDE.

VIEW from West Side.

were needed and the shops and offices displaced by whole-sale firms in the northwest sector required other accommodations. As a result the migration of retail business to the east and south was further stimulated. The process of transforming the Public Square from a village green to a commercial center went on at an increasing tempo. The gaps between the business blocks were steadily filled until by 1865 only the north side of the Square retained the appearance of its original function. Here the new Court House and the rebuilt Presbyterian Church together with a row of older residences, served to remind the city that its Square was once a residential and civic center. But for the rest, the other three sides were now almost entirely devoted to commercial buildings (Figure 60).

By mid-century Superior Street west of the Square was already completely lined by business and office buildings and further development was therefore limited to replacement of older structures. The new buildings were in almost all cases a floor higher than their predecessors, marking an adaptation to the increased activity and higher rental values accompanying expansion (Figures 61 & 62).

The same character soon dominated Ontario Street south of the Square (Figure 63) and it was only a matter of time before the implacable advance of the retail firms would encroach upon the residential streets to the east. The first invasion of these communities of homes came in the mid-1860's with the erection of Case Hall, an auditorium and office building on a site one block east of Public Square on Superior Street. Across the street a number of new business buildings went up before 1870 between the old Hoffman Block and the Second Presbyterian Church (Figure 64).

Figure 59. View of the northwest quadrant of Cleveland c. 1880.

Figure 60. West face of the Public Square in 1870.

Figure 61. Superior Street looking east in 1870.

Figure 62. Superior Street, south side, c.1880.

Figure 63.
Public Square and Ontario Street in 1865.

Figure 64. Superior Street east of Public Square in 1865.

On Euclid Avenue where the fine homes were somewhat more thoroughly entrenched behind the wealth and influence of their owners, the earliest business building was erected near the Square in 1876, but it was quickly followed by many others. In fact, by 1878 this part of Euclid near the Square was flanked on both sides by stores. By the 1880's the famous row of grand houses on Euclid Avenue was confined to the stretch between Clinton and Case Avenue (East 40th). At either end these spacious homes were pressed in upon by the growing shopping centers, one emanating from the Square and the second from Willson Avenue where the railroad had been accompanied by business as well as by manufacturing.

The introduction of the railroads and heavy industry on the one hand and the expansion of the retail districts on the other adversely effected the livability of the town. Virtually all the residential parts of town were ultimately effected, but those located nearest the flats and the railroad lines suffered most seriously. There the by-products of noise and dirt resulted in a steady decline which eventually produced substandard dwellings, overcrowded conditions and uncleanliness. In its developed form this may be seen on a west side street which slopes down to the flats. The unpaved street is flanked by a monotonous row of poor wooden houses closely spaced on lots so small as to preclude yards. The factory and train smoke further depreciated the already low scale of values under such conditions. This particular row was built in the 1880's and was known as "Dutch Hill" (Figure 65). It is typical of many quarters of town where industrial employees lived in the neighborhood of their work.

The disintegration of better protected streets was slower. Of these Euclid Avenue continued to be the finest. The open

Figure 65. "Dutch Hill," c. 1880.

Figure 66. Euclid Avenue, c. 1870.

spaces between the earlier homes were gradually filled in by an orderly procession of stately houses placed deep in the lots on the slight elevation north of the avenue. From this vantage point their front yards sloped gently southward to Euclid Avenue and on the north they had a clear view of the lake. This monumental site was fully exploited by formal spacing and well planned landscaping. The wealthy residents of the street, as Payne has pointed out, lavished great care and considerable funds upon their wide lawns and formal gardens. As leaders of the community they were able also to exert the necessary pressure to ensure properly graded and drained streets, adequate sidewalks and shade trees (Figure 66). At one point they were even able to divert the street railway from their avenue. By such measures the quality of this street was maintained for most of the second half of the century.

Even so the tenure of Euclid Avenue as a handsome residential street was limited. In the face of the forces unleashed by industrialization its fine character was most difficult to maintain. Cut by the railroad at Willson Avenue and grasped in a vise of retail districts it became, as well, an increasingly important traffic artery. By the end of the century its best days were over and today it is almost exclusively a commercial street. Its chief rivals as fashionable residential streets were Prospect and Woodland, Superior east of the Square and St. Clair. By the end of the 1860's each of these bore a street railway and each in its turn succumbed to the inroads of commerce and industry.

In retrospect it may be seen that the chief product of the first decades of industrialization in Cleveland was an accumulating confusion. With no tradition of long-range planning as a guide and ill-served by the motive of economic expediency, the design of the town was year by year more completely dissolved in formlessness. Space was not properly allocated to the several functions of the town and both the definitions of areas and the integration of operations gradually broke down. By a cumulative process a chaotic result was ultimately produced.

The civic problems attendant upon this development mounted proportionately. Extension of the town and the increase in traffic made better surfacing of the streets imperative. Wood planking was no longer adequate. Except in the open country it was almost wholly abandoned and replaced by a wood-block surface known as Nicholson paving. Although this was a vast improvement, it tended to buckle from the effects of frost and required constant repair. Moreover, the loose gravel on which this pavement rested was dirty and washed out in heavy rains, so that repeated efforts were made to discover a cleaner and more durable surface. By 1871 experiments were conducted with coal tar on stone foundations and in the next years macadamized pavement was first used. The introduction to Cleveland of the steam roller in 1872 greatly facilitated the laying of such surfaces.[65]

These expensive pavements were extended slowly. Until the 1880's only the streets in the center of town were provided with such durable surfaces, while the residential areas had to be content with gravelled roads. In fact, a large majority of the streets of town were gravel until almost the end of the century, although a large number of the streets beyond the center were improved by grading and gutters in the early years of the industrial period. The newspapers bear witness to the constant pressure exerted on the council for such minimum improvements, especially during the late 1850's and 1860's.

The problems of street care did not end here, however. With congestion came pressing problems of refuse disposal and drainage of surface water. These two were related and greatly complicated as well by the practice of the times of dumping garbage and other refuse in the gutters. Solutions were sought by two means, the provision of sewers and the initiation of a system of garbage collection. The first underground drains were installed in 1853 but these were few and shallow and soon proved inadequate. By 1860 the demand for an extension of the sewer system reached the proportions of a crusade, and as a result there were 23,116 feet of sewer in Cleveland by 1865. Thereafter efforts were redoubled to provide a coordinated system. The state of the streets rapidly improved in the next decades.[66]

The second aspect of the problem was less quickly solved. Garbage collection was instituted in 1860 but only on a private contract basis which soon proved inadequate. The collections were irregularly made and the refuse continued to accumulate. Tentative experiments with collection by the city were likewise ineffective until regularized and aided by the erection of a disposal plant at the end of the century.

The two public utilities started in the canal period, water supply and gas, were called upon to keep pace with the expansion of the city. With the facilities already in operation to supply gas light to the centrally located streets and buildings, a comparatively small investment was needed to extend this service. Pipes were laid and lights provided in the canal basin and on Pittsburgh, Kinsman and Erie Streets to the south and east by 1855. The west side of the river was supplied in 1857 and in the next year the main streets in the eastern outskirts were lighted.[67]

The water supply proved to be a more difficult problem. The small storage tanks in existence were quickly overtaxed by the expansion of the 1850's. As early in 1851 preliminary plans were under discussion for a capacious reservoir and pumping station to supply water from the lake. The plans were sufficiently mature and the finances arranged by 1854 so that installation could be commenced.[68] The first water was made available from this source in 1856, provided by an intake tower off the mouth of the river, a pumping station in the flats and a reservoir on the west side. Within a decade these works were again inadequate, and of still more serious consequence the pollution of the river by sewage and industrial wastes was rendering the supply unpalatable and dangerous to health. Agitation and plans for a better arrangement finally produced a new intake system placed at a safer distance from shore and to the west of the river mouth. The new pumps and larger engine house were in operation by 1876.

The lateral growth of the city created a need for public transportation on a larger scale. As the distances in town grew, private carriages and public hacks were no longer able to handle the traffic. The first efforts at a solution were the omnibuses, a species of multi-seat vehicle drawn by horses. These were interurban as well as local in 1857 and in subsequent years. The *Directory* of 1863 listed ten lines to outlying villages, starting from various hotels in the center of Cleveland.[69] By 1859, however, agitation commenced in the newspapers for street railways. Numerous reports of this means of transportation in other cities were reaching Cleveland and after much public debate and discussion of regulations, ordinances were drawn and a pilot project was finally commenced in the late months of 1859. This was the East Cleveland Railway Company whose vehicles were drawn by horses on metal tracks and traversed the downtown district from the Railroad Depot to Woodland Cemetery. Others were quickly laid thereafter on Kinsman, Prospect, and St. Clair Streets. They were further extended in the 1860's and 1870's until an efficient network of lines made almost all parts of town accessible (See Figures 61 and 67).

During the canal period no public grounds beyond the original Square had been provided despite the exhortations of the public and of the press. The succeeding era did little better. After industralization with its increasing population and its oppressive conditions of noise and dirt, the need for open space and greenery became still more acute. The areas once available near the center of town had long since been appropriated to other purposes and were privately owned and largely built over. The opportunity to provide an adequate park system for the central area at moderate cost had therefore passed. In the absence of other suitable sites an effort was made in desperation to improve the Public Square for this purpose. Though it was almost surrounded by commercial buildings, it was decided to make it as much of an oasis as possible. In 1856, upon the opening of the new water supply a fountain was erected on the southwest corner and in 1857 the decision was reached to close off the streets which crossed the Square by means of a wooden fence. This stayed in place for a decade until the pressure of commercial interests forced its abandonment. The effort to maintain the Square as a park in the center of the city persisted for many years, however. In 1876 Payne described the artificial waterfall and pool traversed by a rustic bridge which graced the southwest sector, the elaborate fountain in the northwest corner, and a pavilion with a rock garden opposite. The whole was at the time well planted with trees and shrubs (Figure 67). Despite these efforts the struggle was a losing one and by the late 1880's the trees were gone and a few small areas of grass bisected by walks were all that remained.

Even at its best the Public Square was quite insufficient to serve the growing city, and public demand for additional park area recommenced in 1865. As usual progress was slow, and it was not until two years later that the council passed a resolution favoring the new park. An Enabling Act in May of 1869, a commission appointed in 1871, and the final purchase of land in 1873 were all necessary to bring it into actual being. In 1876 Payne refers to Lakeview Park as still unfinished. It was located on the steep bank of the lake above the railroad tracks between Seneca and Erie Streets.[70]

> Summit Street was removed farther from the edge of the bluff, and made a wide, handsome drive the entire length of the park. The face of the bluff was graded and terraced. Trees were planted, rock-work piled up, the numerous springs in the side hill taken up for fountains, the unsightly gullies converted into small lakes fed by a series of cascades. In the course of a year taste, skill, money and labor had wrought a complete revolution. Lake View Park to-day, considering its limited extent, is one of the most attractive spots to be found anywhere in the shape of a public park.
>
> The park now includes nine acres in a long, narrow strip, of which the utmost has been made . . . . Along the entire length, above and below, run broad carriage drives with occasional roads of connection, whilst foot-paths traverse the space in all directions. Between the park and the lake, and separated from the former by an iron railing, are the tracks of the Lake Shore and Michigan Southern and Cleveland and Pittsburgh Railroads . . . . (Figure 68)

Until the acquisition of Wade Park in 1892, situated four miles from the city center, this narrow strip of embankment was the only park on the east side of the river, aside from the Public Square.

With the advent of the railroads and especially of heavy industry, there arose the most serious problem yet to face the municipality. The issues of water supply and lighting, street care and parks, paled beside the difficulties of smoke and water pollution. The policy adopted to solve these problems was no policy at all, but abdication. The conflict of interests which brought this result is clearly indicated in the editorial comment and the news items in the daily papers of the period. Cleveland was fully aware of the contributions being made to prosperity by heavy industry. Nonetheless it was polluting the river and the air and endangering health. There were no established procedures for the control of private enterprise for the public good, so of course, industry went uncurbed. But not before spasmodic efforts had been made to control the menace of smoke and pollution. An editorial in the *Leader* in 1855 when the dangers of the situation were first beginning to be felt is indicative:

> It is yearly becoming a thing more necessary to the comforts of our citizens, that the smoke rolling in such volume out of

Figure 68.
Lakeview Park in 1876.

Figure 67.
Public Square in the 1860's.

the chimneys of our large manufactories should be entirely consumed. We have now in and about our city scores of chimney stacks, that pour out clouds of smoke and soot, producing a great amount of discomfort.

There have been many inventions for affecting this purpose but none of them have ever been entirely acceptable. The invention of Charles Wye Williams, of the Dublin and Liverpool Steam and Navigation Co., has met with the approval of all who have used it, and has been adopted to some extent in this country, but generally in England.

It should be insisted that to every new factory worked by steam (and there is no reason to believe any will be built before long) the furnace should have one of these smoke consumers attached . . . . The cost for putting one into the old establishments would also be very little, and for the sake of comfort and cleanliness it should be done.

This is a sound appraisal of the situation, surprisingly so at such an early date, and legislation to control the problem followed.

But even those few laws which were passed in an effort to control the worst abuses proved abortive in the face of determined opposition. Just as in the earlier period the commercial prosperity of the town was encouraged at the cost of a mercantile slum on the flats and an ill-formed retail area, so now in 1860 any obstruction in the path of industrial progress was ruthlessly opposed. This point of view was stated by the *Leader* of February 7, 1860:

An ordinance has been drawn up by city council allowing no coal oil manufacturing within the city limits. This action should be spiked at once. If coal oil can't be refined in the city no other factory should be allowed to produce in the city.

And again in July of that year a typical editorial appeared:

The Cuyahoga county grand jury has indicated a railroad iron mill company as a nuisance on account of smoky chimneys.

The idea of striking a blow at industry and prosperity of the infant iron manufactories of C. by indicating the most

extensive and important of them all as a nuisance is an act that should and will be reprobated by the whole community.

This campaign apparently succeeded for no abatement of the smoke nuisance is recorded. In 1883 the legislature passed a law empowering the city to regulate the nuisance, but its powers were limited and the effect of the law negligible.

Simultaneously the city was faced with the equally serious pollution of its waters. Ever since they were first installed, the gutters along Cleveland streets had drained directly into the streams or the lake. When the sewers gradually replaced these culverts no change in method of disposal was made and until well into the 1880's all sewers emptied directly into the river and lake from which the Cleveland water supply was drawn.

The uncontrolled dumping of industrial wastes and unconsumed by-products further contaminated the waters. It has been seen that as early as the 1860's the impurity of the lake off the mouth of the river was such that a whole new installation for water supply became necessary. As in the case of smoke control the policy on water pollution was one of evasion. This attiude again had the support of the newspapers. A very revealing editorial was published in the *Leader* on March 5, 1861:

A petition is now before the City Council praying for the repeal of an ordinance, which was passed four years ago, making it unlawful to pour any slops, filth, etc., into the Cuyahoga River within the city limits, and which in effect, shuts off manufactories and refineries from being established upon the river banks. This petition should be granted. To refuse to do it, is to pursue the same policy toward manufactures that has diverted trade and business to other more favorable points, and has greatly retarded the legitimate growth of our city. Our prosperity hereafter will be measured by our manufactures . . . . We need have no fear of Malaria, allowing manufactories to be located upon the river, for its current's strong enough to prevent such an evil . . . .

Pittsburgh is not a pleasant city, but under its dense smoke, and its begrimed atmosphere, it has a substratum of manufactures that will enable it to bid fair defiance to all ordinary panics and dull seasons . . . . Cleveland, on the other hand, indicts her rolling mills because they smoke, and prohibits coal refineries because they smell badly, and gets laughed at by all her sister cities.

Nothing could be clearer than this. Unpleasant though smoke and water pollution might be, these inconveniences had to be endured. Prosperity was more important than the livability of the town. Any curbs upon industry threatened that prosperity and could not be tolerated.

The point of view of this editorial well summarizes the attitudes of the period and is the final clue needed to explain the disintegration which engulfed the city during these industrial decades. Given the undoubted facts that the third quarter of the century inherited an unwieldly city design and an already ill-formed physical structure of buildings; given, too, that the spasm of industrialization introduced too rapidly for absorption the powerful forces of mechanization: nonetheless the ill effects of these conditions might have in good part been mitigated had proper foresight been exercised. But as long as the judgment of the leaders was blinded by a preoccupation with prosperity and as long as the few sporadic efforts at control were effectively thwarted, the chaos and disintegration were virtually inevitable.

The architecture of Cleveland after 1854 was an integral part of this development and reflected in many ways the character of the town. The expansion of the iron and steel industries provided the builders with new structural potentials which effected the form of the building and the advancing technology provided new tools to apply to the traditional building materials. More efficient plumbing and heating systems were developed and a few items of household equipment for washing and cleaning began to appear. As a result of these and other factors, the architectural profession was changing. Though the "master-builder" such as C. W. Heard still held firmly to his position, there were now an increasing number of professionally trained architects. In these circumstances the importance of the carpenter's handbook declined and the cleavage between professional design and the product of the craftsman widened. Provincialism and vernacular style began to disappear and the quality of the average carpenter's work declined. In the design of the professional architect the trend was toward greater flexibility and more spacious arrangements, but the walls and partitions became heavier and surface treatment more massive and ornate. Except in the design of churches which clung to the medieval vocabulary, these tendencies culminated in the awkward but vigorous forms associated with the mansard roof. Thus in general terms the interiors were better equipped and more versatile, reflecting the inventiveness and vitality of the industrial city, but at the same time the designs were the product of its willful but often misdirected energies.

As the establishment of heavy industry, headed by the processing of iron ore, was the most significant factor in the growth of the city after mid-century, so also metal was the most important addition to the materials of construction. Structural iron had been used occasionally for some years in Cleveland, specifically in the iron rods which supported the balconies of several churches in the 1830's. After 1850, when it became available in quantity and as its structural potential was better understood its application to architecture suddenly increased. The cast iron post was soon adopted as a standard member both for interior support and on the facades of commercial buildings at the street level in order to permit larger store fronts of glass. It usually was used in conjunction with a structural wall of masonry. A typical such building is described by the *Leader* in 1855:

It [Payne and Perry's commercial block] is constructed of face brick above the first story, which is supported by iron columns. Heard and Porter were the architects.

The interior supports in the high school completed in 1856 by the same firm were likewise of cast iron, as were those of the Court House two years later. This space-saving, weight-resistant member became standard for almost all large buildings in the decades to follow. In addition, many buildings were remodelled to benefit by its obvious advantages.[71]

The versatility of iron in both cast and wrought form led to its application to a variety of other uses both structural and decorative. In the notice of a new commercial building on Superior Street, the *Leader* on May 18, 1858, states significantly that: "One hundred and sixty square feet of the pavement in front of the building will be made of glass squares eight inches square and one inch thick, set in iron sash." An advertisement in the same paper in 1856 by A. G. Searls, machinist and engineer states his qualifications as a manufacturer of steam engines and "also of iron gratings, railings (cast and wrought), verandas and balconies." These forms attained popularity at once and their character may be seen in a photograph of the Kennard House, to the facade of which they were added largely for their decorative qualities (Figure 69).

The longest step forward in the use of metal was made, however, when girders and I-beams were incorporated into the structural system of the building. The first references to such a radical innovation in a building designed by local architects are to be found in connection with the new Court House of 1858. Great strides in the fabrication of metal had to be made before such a method of construction was possible. The significance of the technological advances did not escape the editorial writers of the time:

Figure 69. Kennard House in 1876.

Messrs. Stone, Chisholm, Jones, and Company of the Newburgh rolling mills have a contract for the heaviest mill castings ever made west of Pittsburgh. The contract includes, six solid iron rolls weighing four and one-half tons each of the proper dimensions for rolling out beams, joists, rafters, and other wrought iron fixtures required for the new court house.

The Cleveland Rolling mill employs 125 men . . . . We should remark that in filling the contract for the new court house in this city this company has made beams 24 feet long, four feet longer than any ever made in this country outside New York city.[72]

With this kind of material available, the versatility of iron in both cast and wrought form was further exploited. In a description of this same Court House just prior to its completion the *Leader* included the statement that:

There are forty tons of iron stairways in the building. A circular gallery extends from the first floor to the roof. Labor and materials for this immense building comes from Cleveland Mechanics, with the exception of the corrugated iron roofing which comes from Pittsburgh . . . . All the floors above the basement are of iron paved in concrete.

These quotations reflect great pride in the achievements of local "mechanics," and it is true that the development of the Cleveland iron industry was a prerequisite to such construction in the city. But the structural methods employed were not new. The development of structural forms in cast and wrought iron started as early as the 18th century and became increasingly important during the next decades, particularly in England. To judge by the descriptions, the system of construction used in the Cleveland Court House was similar to that developed by Watt and Boulton in the Salford Mill, Manchester, in 1801. Here for the first time cast iron I-beams supported on columns formed an internal skeleton incorporated within outer masonry walls and with floors erected upon brick arches. A generation later this primitive system was given a firmer foundation by the researches of William Fairbairn. After numerous tests of cast and wrought iron members of various shapes Fairbairn published his results in a small volume in 1854.[73]. There he describes in considerable detail the system he had perfected, and provides drawings and tables to assist the architect in using his inventions. He employed cast iron columns and wrought iron I beams, having established the greater strength and lightness of the wrought metal for this purpose in his elaborate tests. These beams were connected by tie-rods. The floors were supported either on brick arches or on iron plates bent in the form of a segmental arch. In either case the spandrels above the arches were leveled by concrete fill and the floors of the next story laid thereon. He rightly considered this system a major contribution to the art of construction by reason of its strength, and hence expected it to be particularly applicable to factories and warehouses.

A comparable system of construction was first developed in this country by Bogardus in the 1840's. He, however, eliminated the masonry wall (common to Watt's and Fairbairn's methods) in favor of a complete iron frame. This gave him an exterior facing as well as interior supports of iron. He also replaced Fairbairn's iron tie-rods with exposed decorative girders which span the space between columns and form part of the ceiling design of the finished interior. Otherwise Bogardus' methods are similar to the English ones. Brick arches carried on I-beams support the floor above, and the membering of the structure is essentially the same. Bogardus hoped to produce a strong and fireproof building dependent exclusively on the flexible new material of iron, and his innovations set in motion a widespread use of these materials in this country.

These new ideas in building appear to have reached Cleveland in the late 1850's. The Federal Building, located on Public Square on the site of the Leonard Case house, was designed for Cleveland in 1856 by Ammi B. Young, the official architect for the United States Treasury. His design for Cleveland was published in 1856 as one of a series of pamphlets, and shows that in the Federal Building he adopted the system of iron construction for the whole interior structure. His cast iron columns carried built-up girders of oblong section which in turn supported I-beams. The latter were cross-braced by tie rods ingeniously designed to hook over the rounded upper member of the I-beam. The brick arches and concrete fill were used in the usual way to form the floors. Wood furring, however, was also carried by the I-beams, and wood strips were sunk in the concrete above, permitting regulation wooden floors and plaster ceilings to be fitted to this skeleton of iron. By this system Young was able to design a building which had all the structural advantages of the metal frame while it retained the internal appearance of traditional wooden or masonry construction. The exterior bearing walls were of stone, also, and so as far as its appearance is concerned, the Federal Building was a traditional structure.

The first locally designed building to use this metal interior structure was the New Court House built in 1858 when the Federal Building was still under construction. The frequent notices of this building in local newspapers as already noted refer to the use of wrought-iron beams, castings, and floors of iron paved in concrete. A photograph of this building during demolition bears this out also for the fallen columns and I-beams may be seen (Figure 70).

Unlike the pioneering designs of Bogardus, neither the Federal Building nor its local contemporary, the Court House, abandoned the solid exterior walls of masonry construction. Nor did they use the exposed interior girders of the Harper's Building in New York. For all their innovations in construction, therefore, these buildings did not reflect the new materials in their surface treatment.

Figure 70. New Court House under demolition.

Figure 71.
Union Passenger Depot in 1876.

The most spectacular advance in building design made possible by the fabrication of structural iron came in the enclosure of spaces of a size hitherto impractical. In Cleveland this new possibility was most fully exploited in the Union Passenger Depot, erected in 1864-6 (Figure 71). This building had an interior space of 603 by 180 feet under a single roof. The 24-inch exterior walls were of conventional masonry but the roof supports and anchorage depended upon metal. In the absence of drawings or photographs of the interior, the best description of this structure is a contemporary one in the *Leader* on November 5, 1866:

> The stupendous roof is supported by 49 iron trusses weighing nearly 400 tons. It is anchored down by means of strong iron rods fastened firmly to the walls below.

In this building which enclosed the largest space to that date attempted in Cleveland, the possibilities of the new materials which accompanied industrialization reached their most satisfactory fruition in this period.

The technology of the period was applied as well to the processing of the older materials. Traditional American ingenuity was immensely stimulated by the possibilities of iron, and machines for shaping stone and wood were constantly improved. An interesting notice in the *Leader* on June 27, 1857, would indicate that the improving technology even led to an experiment with partial prefabrication:

> A Kentucky gentleman came to the city a short time ago in search of a "portable store house" all the necessary timbers morticed and otherwise ready to place in an upright position.
> Messrs. Kennedy and Smith shipped the timber, shingles and hardware to the man in the remarkable time of four days. When put together the building will be 25 feet by 40 feet and two stories high, with a fashionable store front.

There is, of course, no evidence that such methods were either commonly employed or their potentialities further developed in this period.

At the same time great improvements in the mechanical equipment of buildings were introduced. In particular, better facilities for heating and washing were developed and installed in many of the finer buildings. In 1857 the owners of the Angier House put in a "new steam heating apparatus designed for washing clothes, ironing and drying, cooking, heating rooms, etc."[74] The new Court House of 1858 and later public buildings were equipped with central heating systems, as were several of the churches and schools. Even the more expensive private homes had elaborate installations for bathing and heating. The *Leader* of January 28, 1858, included in its detailed description of the famous residence for Amasa Stone these items: a fireproof furnace with heated air piped to each room, a boiler attached to this furnace for heating water which also had outlets in most rooms, and a model laundry connected with a cistern for soft water. These unheard-of conveniences were becoming available for the first time in these decades and ultimately changed the whole concept of minimum standards of comfort in American architectural design.

Contributions to this new standard were also made by the invention of household appliances, in which the manufacturers took considerable pride, as the *Leader* noted on December 30, 1858:

> A recent Ohio patent for a washing machine was issued to F. B. Pratt and F. Tyler of Cleveland. This invention claims superiority over other machines of the kind.
> This is an age of invention, and among the machines that are constantly astonishing the world is a carpet sweeper. Five minutes inspection will show its construction. Ladies are invited to call and examine it at Barnum's sewing machine depot on Superior St. The price is three dollars.

Stylistic changes accompanied these innovations, but at a somewhat slower pace. The development of iron and more versatile machinery radically changed the internal structural system and introduced many conveniences. It made possible new interior space and flexibility and to that extent modified overall proportions. But exterior design responded more slowly to the new possibilities. The practice of designing in terms of masonry and in accepted "styles" was too deeply entrenched to be easily abandoned. In fact, after mid-century a marked tendency to uniformity in the stylistic character of Cleveland architecture of whatever building type becomes apparent. Before the end of this period the so-called "French" style had eclipsed all previous fashions except in the churches.

Several circumstances seem to have contributed to this not altogether happy result. The technical problems involved in the use of structural metal and in the erection of larger and more flexible buildings called for advanced training on a professional level. This was provided by two sources. First, the older, self-trained master builders, such as C. W. Heard, attained through long experience with important buildings the necessary proficiency in structural methods. Secondly, in this period the evidence shows that an increasing proportion of the practising architects were receiving formal training in their profession.[76] These two groups of men alone had the technical skill to design major buildings, both public and private, and the activities of the carpenters were in consequence largely confined to small frame buildings. In these circumstances the contributions to architectural design previously made by the craftsman were lost. The naive and original forms of the vernacular no longer affected style.

The economic conditions attendant upon industrialization widened this gulf between the architect and craftsman. The small houses built by the carpenter were still the larger proportion of the actual structures in the town but their quality had markedly declined. They had to be produced in large numbers and at minimum cost to house the increasing population.[77] As exemplified by "Dutch Hill," they were buildings of nondescript character without architectural significance. The cleavage between the fashionable and the poor districts of town was sharpened by this division

between the art of the architect and that of the carpenter.

Provincialism was equally on the decline in Cleveland and had in fact almost disappeared as early as 1840. The railroad and mass immigration tied the midwest firmly to the rest of the country, and the importation of architects brought the latest fashions to Cleveland. For this reason the carpenter's manual became less important as a source for design. The vernacular forms which it supplied could no longer compete with fashionable styles developed by leading innovators. By the 1860's this formal art was to be dominated by the mansard roof, designated the "French" style.

The "French" manner was fashionable, but there were other and more pertinent reasons for its popularity. The desire for more space and a greater variety of functions, both in public buildings and expensive residences, required new forms. The high ceilings and large windows which were in demand were easily accommodated to the style. It was therefore to a certain extent a functional form, adapted to contemporary needs. But equally the adoption of the French form was a matter of taste. The restless energy of the period seems to be reflected in its vigorous masses and bulky forms; the disorderly growth of the town has its counterpart in the ill-controlled vitality of its heavy detail. It was responsive to the trends of the times.

For these various reasons architecture changed more completely at this time than at any previous period. The simple surfaces of the canal period gradually gave way to quoins and rustication, attached pilasters and projecting eaves. The size of brackets doubled and the silhouette of the building was broken by irregular masses. Wall thickness was increased sometimes to as much as 24 inches. Windows were high and narrow and ceiling heights were raised to 13 or 15 feet so that the new buildings towered over their older neighbors. Together with the greater overall size and the variety of interior arrangements, these changes brought into being an almost entirely new architecture before the end of this period. To construct these massive buildings cut stone was soon found to be the most appropriate of the traditional materials, and wood and brick were less and less favored as the period advanced.

Unlike the canal period, the succeeding era required a number of government buildings. The old Court House which had served since 1828 was no longer adequate. A new post office and custom house for the activities in Cleveland of the Federal government was needed; the city finally decided to erect a city hall after being inadequately served since its founding by rented quarters in commercial buildings. Also associated with this group of buildings was Case Hall, built as a private enterprise by Leonard Case, but semi-public in its functions, which included a public auditorium and rooms for the library association.

The location of these various new buildings presented certain difficulties. By the time they were built, in the late 1850's and thereafter, the Public Square had been almost pre-empted by commerce. Except for the north side and one site on the east, it was surrounded by business blocks. No other centrally located site for a unified civic center was available. As a result these new public buildings were located wherever space could be found in the general vicinity of the Square. The only two positions open on the Square itself were used: the Court House was situated on the north side next to the Presbyterian Church and the Federal Building replaced the old Leonard Case homestead on the east. The City Hall, however, had to be located a block away on the north side of Superior Street with Case Hall beside it. In 1875 when a fourth court house was needed, it was relegated to Seneca Street and the city jail and police court were built on Champlain. Thus the unity which should have characterized the civic functions of the town was impossible and the monumental government buildings erected were shorn of their effectiveness by dispersion. A unified group design for the public buildings of Cleveland had to await the Group Plan of 1905.

Of these public buildings the new Court House and the Federal Building arose together. The former was commenced in February of 1858 and completed in a little over two years. Its thick exterior walls of brick with stone facing, its heavy interior dividing walls which carried I-beams, and its use of cast iron columns and concrete and iron floors have already been noted. The view of the building during demolition reveals in addition the central well which rose through the three floors and was surrounded by a continuous staircase, an open feature which exploited the structural possibilities of iron (see Figure 70). Nothing on the exterior, however, suggested the use of the new materials within, as has been seen. Rather, the four-square solidity of the building reflects only the masonry bearing walls and the architectural detail is historical in derivation. Though it was described as "Romanesque" by the *Leader* at the time, it has rather a Renaissance or Italianate character in the use of quoins at the corners on the lower level and of a balcony over the entrance and cornice and pediment above (Figure 72). This was the design of a local architect by the name of J. J. Husband, and it is one of the most satisfactory buildings of the period in its simple proportions and sheer wall treatment.

The Federal Building diagonally across the Square was built during the same years. The indecision created by the commercial dominance of the Square is indicated by the long debate in the newspapers over the choice of a site for this building. Such diverse locations were suggested as the corner of Superior Lane and Vineyard, Bank and Water Streets, and Seneca Street, as well as the site finally chosen. As has been seen, this building was designed by Ammi B. Young as one of a large number of government buildings needed to serve the Federal activities which accompanied the expansion of the western towns before

Figure 72. New Court House.

Figure 73. Federal Building in 1876.

Figure 74.
Federal Building in 1900.

Figure 76. Case Hall, c.1900.

the Civil War. They incorporated important structural innovations as outlined above, and in exterior design had a solid Italianate character and severity of design appropriate to their status as emissaries of the national government. In the Cleveland example the bold mouldings, heavy cornice and five bay design of the windows are particularly satisfying (Figure 73). Large wings were added to the Federal Building in the 1880's without destroying its character (Figure 74). These were two of the last public buildings in this period to escape the mansard roof.

The next important public building, Case Hall, was the first in Cleveland to employ the mansard roof, inaugurating a practice which was persistently followed thereafter. It stood immediately behind the Federal Building on Superior Street and became a familiar land-mark in the center of town. The building was first contemplated and its excavation started in 1859. Many notices in the papers trace its slow and interrupted progress before the *Leader* could state in September of 1865 that:

> The $200,000 Case Building, in the rear of the post office, is nearing completion. The architects are Hurd [Heard] and Blythe. It was commenced in 1859, and, during the first year of the war no work was done on it. The ground floor consists of store rooms. The second is for offices. The Cleveland Library association will occupy rooms on the second floor. The building is of red brick, trimmed with stone, with a French roof. It is 76 by 200 feet.

The hall was not actually in use until September of 1867 according to Payne who published a print of its initial appearance (Figure 75). In style this building stands midway between the earlier Court House and the City Hall, which was to follow. The wall surfaces are interrupted at intervals by quoins and pilasters and by horizontal string-courses at the lower levels. The cornice is borne on deep brackets and the dormer windows and chimneys compli-

*Figure 75.
Case Hall in 1876.*

Figure 77. City Hall in 1876.

Figure 78. Union Passenger Depot, c.1900

cate the silhouette of the roof. Though it is a well proportioned and sharply designed building, these tendencies to ornamented surfaces and bulky forms indicate the direction of taste in these years. It stood until 1902 when both Case Hall and the Federal Building were taken down to make way for a new post office. A late photograph reveals that Case underwent some remodelling after its original construction, particularly in the enlargement of windows on the ground floor and at the fourth floor level (Figure 76).

The "French" style was finally triumphant in the ambitious City Hall completed in 1875 (Figure 77). It rose through five stories including the top floor within the mansard roof and had a sixth level in the tower. The street floor was given over to stores but the rest of the building contained the many offices of the city administration together with a council chamber twenty feet high with a public gallery. This occupied the upper two floors. The exact disposition of these rooms is described in detail by Payne and he further states that it was equipped with the most modern facilities including "A steam elevator which connects all the floors." Here at last was the fully formed "French" style which was to be found again in the principal hotel, several business blocks, and the late residences of the period. Its characteristics were fairly uniform in all building types: The windows were large and closely spaced for maximum light. They were separated vertically by heavy pilasters with boldly-cut capital forms, and horizontally by equally massive string courses. The areas of plain wall surface have, in consequence, disappeared. The cornice of the building was supported by large brackets in two sizes, and the mansard roof was broken at intervals by dormer windows. A further bold irregularity was achieved by a variety of roof heights, massive chimneys and elaborate ornament on the edges of the roof forms. The whole design was characterized by that quality of misdirected energy which pervades the town as a whole under the impetus of industrialization.

The designers of this period were quick to grasp the new possibilities offered by fabricated iron. When they were faced with a new architectural problem such as that of a train shed and passenger station, they arrived at a forthright solution. The new railroad terminal was well described by Payne:[78]

> The Union Passenger Depot, situated on the lake shore, at the foot of Bank and Water Streets, is one of the most substantial, commodious and well arranged buildings of its kind in the country. It is convenient of access, being but ten minutes walk from the Post Office, and five to eight minutes from the principal hotels, with which it is connected by lines of street railroad. The edifice was erected in 1865, and is built entirely of stone and iron. Its length is six hundred and three feet, and width one hundred and eighty feet, and it contains four thousand two hundred and fifty feet of track. Is complete in all its appointments, having large and well furnished ticket, express and telenews depot, and numerous offices for the use of the officers of the road in all the various departments.

The print which accompanied this description and a later photograph of the building in its original state give its exterior appearance (Figure 78). The southern section throughout its length, including the tower, housed the offices and facilities described by Payne. This enormous shed originally enclosed a space which would have been virtually impossible without the iron trusses employed. The new problem was treated in a forthright manner by the designer. He emphasized the interior proportions by the extended sloping planes of the side roofs and the flattened arch which crowns the building. Since his structural system permitted it, he used a continuous line of clerestory windows. The compartmentation of the south portion was suggested by the blind arcade on the east end and the small windows along the south wall together with the row of chimneys in the roof above. The only concession to conventional design was the rusticated and arcaded treatment of the stone walls and tower. This building represents the longest step yet taken in Cleveland toward the full exploitation of the new materials.

The commercial buildings of the time followed much the same evolution as those built for government functions. They abandoned the simple surfaces and block forms of the canal period in favor of the heavy ornament and massive forms of the mansard style. With their high ceilings and added stories these new buildings towered above their older neighbors. They were too distinctive in both style and proportions to be incorporated easily into the older pattern, and in fact gave to the retail district an even more disjointed design than it already had. Thus, far from serving as a unifying influence, the characteristics of the mansard design contributed to the confusion cultivated by industrialization.

Since few hotels were built in Cleveland in this period, the whole evolution of the style cannot be traced in this form of building. The only two important hotels built after 1854 provide instead a contrast between the early and late characteristics. The Angier House, built in 1855 and later called the Kennard House, was closely related to the style of the Weddell house (See Figure 69). Its significance for the industrial period lies in the use of iron balconies on the facade and particularly in the modern installations which have already been noted. The contrast is provided by the additions to the Forest City House made at the end of this period. Although this part of the hotel was undertaken as a remodelling and extension of the old Dunham House in the 1870's, the new portion of the hotel was so radically different from the older building as to constitute an entirely new structure. In the two views the old building stands on the corner of Superior and the Square with the new section to its left, dominated by the usual tower

and mansard roof (Figures 79 and 80). The greater interior space of this addition is indicated by the fact that although it had the same number of floors, it towers far above the original building. The contrast in the exterior wall treatment is equally striking. The plain brick walls and paneled design of the old building contrast with the quoined and pilastered forms, the stringcourses, enframed windows and massive roof of the new addition.

In the stores which were built after 1854 some of the intermediate steps may be seen. A photograph of the east side of Ontario Street opposite the end of Champlain shows the variations of style which developed from 1855 to about 1860 (Figure 81). The earliest building of this group is probably the one on the right. The unframed windows and minimum cornice are characteristic of the simplicity found in the 1850's. The increased height of the floors in the left-hand buildings indicate a later date, and the arched windows surmounted by a curved moulding may be found as late as the 1870's in some building types. Despite these changes in detail the whole group has the plain surfaces of the pre-mansard taste.

The change to the heavy forms in retail store design came after 1860. Early in this decade the E. I. Baldwin Building on Superior Street was erected (See Figure 22). It was among the earliest in the new style. The solid window enframement, the stringcourses and the decorated mansard roof are typical of the times. Thereafter these were to be the common characteristics of commercial building. It is to be noted that in this building for the first time almost the entire front wall consists of windows. Cast iron posts on the street floor enframe large panes of glass and support the masonry above, and the Gothic windows on the upper floors are separated only by heavy mullions. Thus the bulky detail did not interfere with a more open facade which constituted an important improvement in the convenience of the design. This too became an identifying feature of the succeeding buildings. In the A. D. Herenden

Figure 80. Forest City House, c.1880.

Figure 79. Forest City House in 1876.

Figure 81. Ontario Street, c.1860.

Figure 83. Brownell Street School in 1876.

Figure 82. Herenden Building in 1876.

Building of 1869 on Bank Street the best and worst features of the style in its final form are summarized[79] (Figure 82—see also Figure 25).

As in the period of the canals, the expanding city encountered great difficulty in providing schools for the mounting number of children. Payne outlines the troubles of the school board in this matter:[80]

> So rapid is the increase of demand for school facilities, that although the work of erecting large and costly buildings goes on continuously the supply keeps far behind the demand; the new buildings are crowded as soon as completed, and it becomes necessary in every case to supplement the new brick "educational palaces" with a number of frame "relief buildings", until another structure can be built. The report for the school year ending August 31, 1876, shows there were in operation that year 24 grammar and primary schools and 5 schools of higher grade.

By reason, perhaps, of these pressures which taxed to the utmost the budget alloted to school construction, the design of the city's school buildings was persistently conservative. There was a natural tendency to establish a serviceable and inexpensive type and to repeat it many times. This led to a simple form of building with a minimum of ornament. As a consequence the ornate forms which infected other types were not applied to school buildings in Cleveland until almost 1870. The first such design was that of the St. Clair Street School erected in 1868.

The "Bradburn" type," represented by the Kentucky School, was retained until 1855. By that time a larger building became imperative and the nine-room design of the Eagle School was built and frequently repeated.[81] It was a simple oblong building of two stories, but compared to the earlier buildings it had a professional stamp and was in fact the first school to be designed by a trained architect. Its bracket-supported cornice and arched window mouldings were very similar to those of contemporary commercial buildings. It was not replaced as a standard design until the Brownell Street (East 14th) School was built in 1865 (Figure 83). This was once again an enlarged design, having an additional floor and a total of eighteen rooms. Otherwise this building was very similar to its predecessor on Eagle Street, having the simple surfaces and a minimum of ornament which were least expensive to build.[82]

The earliest departure from this rule of simplicity which had controlled the design of Cleveland's schools since the first Academy of 1821 was the Central High School Building completed in 1856 (Figure 84). During the development of its design the arrangement of the rooms on each floor was several times changed, the final disposition being thus described by the *Leader* in September, 1855:

> We point with pleasure and pride to the new high school now nearing completion on Euclid St. opposite the Baptist church. The building is of the Romanesque style of architecture; it is faced with sandstone and is 45 feet high. The first floor will contain school rooms and a library; the second floor a school room, two recitation rooms and a philosophical apparatus room; the third floor is divided into a hall 58 x 75 feet, and an apparatus room. The basement contains three furnace rooms — one for each story. Heard and Porter were the architects.

Freese published a cut of the building which was made at the time of its completion in 1856 and which reveals that here for the first time in Cleveland the elements of an historical style were applied to a school building. Though advertised as "Romanesque," it would be more accurate to describe it as a hybrid of medieval forms, predominantly Gothic in character. The paired chimneys, the turrets and crenellations, and the steep gable all belong to that style as practised in these decades. The slender, octagonal turrets which flanked the central pavilion were comparable to those used by the same firm on the Second Presbyterian Church of a few years earlier. The high and

*Figure 85.
Central High School in 1900.*

Figure 84. Central High School, 1856.

narrow windows of the upper floors reflect the spacious ceiling heights inside. The main body of the building was of brick but the basement and facade were faced with cut stone and cast iron columns supported the floors on the interior. This was a spacious and flexible building and served its purpose well for over twenty years as a public library after being relinquished by the school board. A photograph taken just before it was torn down shows it much as it appeared in the print of 1856 except that two bays have been added on the front and the crenellations at the roof line have been removed (Figure 85).

The end of this period is represented by the 1868 design for the St. Clair School, one of four built on this pattern by Heard and Blythe (Figure 86). In plan these buildings were not unlike the Brownell Street School which immediately preceded them, but the new design was more flexible by reason of a system of cross corridors and corresponding exist. Each room had doorways near the staircases which facilitated movement and made for a safer building. A larger number of windows, particularly in the rooms in the center of the building which had only one exterior wall, provided better light than the older design. All these buildings were heated by steam. In exterior appearance they conform to the new taste. The windows are pointed in the Gothic manner and the entrances and corridors are marked on the exterior by thick buttresses which give the facades a bold plastic character. The silhouette is broken up by massive forms including a double-sloped hipped roof, heavy chimneys and gables. Again in this building the new taste for bulky forms was accompanied by great strides in the utility and convenience of the building.

The pressures of mercantile activity continued to drive the residential sections of town with their churches and schools eastward during the industrial period. Of the many new houses of worship of all sects which arose in response to the needs of the enlarged community, a majority were built in the outer periphery of the town. None of them adopted the "French" style. Rather, they clung to the tested medieval forms, predominately the Gothic. The earliest ones built after 1854 were simple designs with large areas of plain wall surface and square, uncluttered shapes. As the period progressed, there was a marked tendency toward heavier forms and bolder ornament, and toward enlarged and over-decorated interiors. Thus the changing taste infected the religious buildings as well as the secular.

Of the four churches which will demonstrate this evolution, the earliest was the Euclid Avenue Presbyterian located on the corner of Brownell Street. It was begun in 1853 but progressed slowly and was not completed until late in 1859 (Figure 87). Like other structures of the late 1850's it retains the general character of the earlier period. The details of buttresses and pinnacles and the form of the spire all are related to the Upjohn types found in the canal era. It has, too, the plain expanses of wall and dominant square tower of the earlier style. A curious feature, possibly a belfry, is the diagonally situated open arch at the exterior corner of the main nave.

The new church for the Trinity congregation was a finer building (Figure 88). It was erected in 1854-5 to replace the old church of 1828 which burned in the former year. The site chosen was on Superior Street two blocks east of the Square which was still an avenue of homes at that date. It was designed by Ingham, a professional architect from Pittsburgh and constructed at a cost of $30,000, and served the community until 1902 when the present Trinity Cathedral was occupied.[83] Compared to contemporary churches this building had a professional quality. The walls were smooth-faced cut stone and the character of the details was heavy and sharply cut. Twin entrances were placed at the corners of the main facade on either side of the bay housing the organ which was dominated by a

Figure 86. St. Clair Street School, 1868.

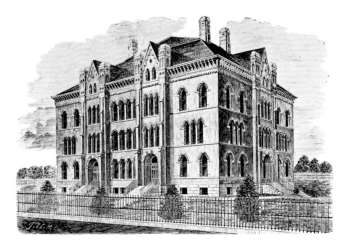

Figure 87. Euclid Avenue Presbyterian Church, 1853-1859.

Figure 88. Trinity Church, 1854-1855.

large, authentically Gothic window. The curiously dwarfed tower which surmounted the gable seems out of scale with the other features of this facade. Payne's detailed description is useful in visualizing the interior of the building:[84]

> The interior is in keeping with the exterior design, and is well arranged and handsome. The nave is one hundred feet by fifty-two feet, and is divided by a wide alley along the middle, the side alleys running close to the wall. The chancel, which is elevated four steps above the floor of the church, is about twenty-five square, and opens into the nave by a lofty arch. At the other extremity of the church is a well arranged organ loft in a recess, flanked by the entrance porches; it opens to the nave by three arches, one of which is filled up by the handsome tracery of the organ case, which occupies one side of the gallery, so as to leave unobscured the elaborately decorated west window. The chancel window is a triplet, filled with rich devices, and the windows of the nave, six on each side, are of two bays each, filled with stained glass. The interior of the church is ornamented in polychrome, executed in 1873. The ceiling of the nave is of cobalt blue, divided into panels about eight feet square. The dark wood-work separating the panels is tastefully decorated with gilt tracings.

This polychromy and the dark woodwork added in 1873 was, of course, consistent with the coloristic and incrusted facades of the 1870's (Figure 89).

The only other church erected at the center of town was the new building for the congregation of Old Stone, the First Presbyterian Society (Figure 90). The old church was torn down in 1853 and the cornerstone for its successor laid on the same site on September 9 of that year. On March 7, 1857, the building was seriously burned shortly after its completion and its interior had to be entirely rebuilt, though the exterior walls of brick and stone erected by that experienced mason, W. J. Warner, were preserved. Thus the exterior form of the building dates from 1853 though the edifice was not completed until

Figure 89. Trinity Church interior in 1890.

1858.[85] The spire of the east tower was finished a decade later and removed after a second fire of 1884. It was never rebuilt. The exterior shell of this building is all that remains of the original construction, having withstood two fires. In this partially preserved condition Old Stone Church is the sole remnant on the Public Square of the buildings which surrounded that park during the first three quarters of the 19th century. All of its predecessors and contemporaries have given way to higher and more modern structures dedicated to the commerce of the contemporary city. Hedged in by skyscrapers and blackened by the smoke of the near-by industry, it is difficult to appraise the quality of this landmark of the 1850's (Figure 91). As its history suggests, it is a solidly constructed building of massive walls which were ornamented with round headed openings and Romanesque detail. Its interior arrangements after the first fire of 1857 may be appraised by the description written by Payne in 1876:[86]

> The interior of the church is divided into three aisles. The ceiling of the main aisle is a groined arch. [sic] The side aisles have each a semi-arched ceiling, also groined. The ceilings and walls are neatly frescoed, the prevailing color being a neutral tint. The pulpit forms an oval. The arched recess at the back is frescoed with four round-headed arches, above which is a band from which are carried lines meeting in a circular false opening, through which flutters a dove. At the sides of the pulpit are massive candelabra with black walnut pedestals. The main body of the church is lighted by eight small pendant chandeliers, four on each side. There are two side galleries, and an organ loft at the entrance end of the church.

Figure 90. Old Stone Church before removal of the east spire.

Figure 91. Old Stone Church, c.1940.

Figure 92. Second Baptist Church in 1876.

This would seem to be a relatively restrained interior scheme compared to the ornateness of the refinishing of Trinity in 1873, which may provide a measure of the change in taste in the intervening decade and one-half.

The last significant church in this period was constructed between 1868 and 1871 on Euclid Avenue at Huntington Street (East 18th) for the Second Baptist Society (Figure 92). Like so many of its predecessors this building no longer exists, having been removed to make way for business buildings. Payne must therefore be relied upon once again for a contemporary description:[87]

> It is generally conceded to be one of the finest ecclesiastical buildings in the city. Its style is the modernized Romanesque. The exterior dimensions of the church and chapel are one hundred and fifty-five feet by sixty-four feet. The tower is twenty feet square at the base, and the height of the lightning rod on the spire is two hundred and thirty-six feet. The front of the building on Euclid Avenue and the side on Huntington Street are of sandstone; the west side of the church and chapel is of red brick with sandstone trimmings. The spire is of wood with slate covering.

Particularly in the tower of this church the propensity for heavy ornamental forms which have their counterpart in the mansard style in secular design may be seen. The surfaces are repeatedly interrupted by buttresses and string-courses. The proportions have a ponderous character and the awkward relationship of masses bespeak a decline in taste. The interior, as described by Payne, must have given the same effect:

> The seats and wainscotings are of black walnut, as also is the chancel furniture. The organ and choir gallery measures seventeen by fifty-four feet. The front, of heavy paneled and molded black walnut, extends across the room and is supported by molded brackets. The front of the pulpit platform is also of paneled walnut . . . . The ceiling is arched,

finished with open timber, cut and molded hammer beams, resting on stone corbels, [sic] molded rafters, purlines, [sic] and paneled moldings.

Despite this somber taste in interior design this was a very convenient building. The subsidiary parts were highly complex and adaptable, according to the description of Payne:

> In the rear of the auditorium are the pastor's study, dressing rooms, private entrance from each dressing room to the baptistry, provided with screen doors on the platform to be used during the time of immersion, and there is also a private exit from each dressing room through the chapel to the street. From the church, directly at the end of each side aisle, entrance is made through two doors into the pastors' study and the dressing rooms, and from these into the chapel and ladies parlors. The main entrance to the chapel and study is from Huntington Street into a large hall, with two flights of stairs on each side, leading to the main and infants' school rooms, Bible-class rooms, and the school library. The chapel can also be entered from Euclid Avenue. The chapel is thirty-five by thirty-six feet, and is connected with the parlors by double doors. The infants' school room overhangs the main school room as a gallery. Sliding glass doors close it in when used as a class room and open it to communicate with the main room during the general exercises.

Such variegated arrangements had never hitherto been made to house the activities of a congregation in Cleveland. Though the taste declined, a compensating gain was made both in the convenience and in the variety of various internal arrangements.

Finally the trend in fashionable and expensive houses was along similar lines. The overall form of the Italian Villa style was still used during the late 1850's, but significant changes were made in its detail. In 1855, Heard and Porter erected a $13,000 mansion for H. B. Hurlburt on

Figure 93. Hurlburt House, 1855.

Euclid Avenue (Figure 93). In a photograph in the Western Reserve Historical Society it may be seen that this house retained the square block of the Italian manner with its characteristic projections and its central cupola. To the familiar ornament of this style have now been added, however, a textured surface of colored brick and elaborate metal ornaments at the various roof lines. The result is a more ornate and sumptuous effect than the simple forms of the original style permitted, a clear indication of a change in taste. Such designs as this one were known as "Oriental Villas" at the time. The lavish adornment was sometimes of a quite exotic character, even including a turnip dome over the cupola. Several designs of this type are to be found in the publications of Samuel Sloan in this same period.

Although the same overall arrangement is used in the residence for Amasa Stone built in 1858, the exterior effect of this building is quite different (Figure 94). The architect has succeeded in obliterating the simple shapes of the Italian villa by his elaborate handling of the forms and surfaces. The facade is divided into bold projecting bays flanking the porch and covered balcony. The plain wall surfaces have disappeared in the heavy window enframement and the recessed niches at each floor level. The brackets supporting widely projecting eaves have been doubled in size, and the silhouette of the building is complicated by heavy stone ornaments in the shape of vases. Within the limits of the Italian villa form this is about as far as the architect could go toward ornate and massive design.

This house was the residence of one of the town's leading industrialists and it received generous notice in the papers. The description by the *Leader* on January 28, 1858 adds pertinent information on this famous residence:

Figure 94. Amasa Stone House, 1858.

The most prominent among the costly residences which have made our city, particularly Euclid St., so famous is that of Amasa Stone, jr. The exterior is a massive structure, with over 700,000 brick being used.

The style of its architecture is regarded as an American style. The main building is 50 x 60 feet, with two projections, one on each side. The height of its stories is 15 and 13 feet respectively. The wing of the building is 27 by 47 feet. The entire partitions and walls are of brick. The exterior walls are 23 inches in thickness, with a hollow space of eight inches to protect the interior of the building from the constant changes of the atmosphere.

The ceilings of the parlor and library are of recess, panel, and cornice work, and have a most handsome effect. The staircase in the hall is finished in mahogany. The newel posts, balusters, and railing, and the doors of the parlor, reception room, and library are finished with rose wood; those of the other apartments are of oak. From the hall door is the view of the second hall floor, by means of an oval opening in the ceiling. The roofs are of tin and thoroughly painted. The furnace is fireproof, being solidly encased in brick and stone work, designed to convey, by means of requisite pipes, heated air over the entire building.

Attached to the furnace is a capacious boiler for heating water. A supply of hot and cold water is found in nearly every apartment.

The portion of the floor covering the furnace is of English encaustic tiling. The entire basement is constructed of stone and brick. In the rear of the basement is the wing basement which is fitted up as a model laundry and fuel room. Connected with the laundry is a pipe leading to a large cistern, by means of which soft water can always be had . . . . It is the finest, the most complete and convenient residence west of Hudson.

To be noted in this contemporary description are the massively thick and insulated walls, the dark paneled interiors and the height and flexibility of the rooms. Particularly of interest are the modern plumbing and heating

Figure 95. Kitchens House, 1860.

Figure 96. Rockefeller House, 1868.

installations which constitute one of the major contributions to the improvement of domestic architectural design stemming from this period. Very few houses in town could equal the luxury of this expensive mansion, but it is interesting to see what the latest technical improvements could produce at this time when the opportunity was presented.

A much more conservative house was built on Euclid Avenue in the next years and later occupied by H. W. Kitchens (Figure 95). It is characteristic of a large number of houses dating from about 1860 some of which still stand on the streets of the city. One of its distinguishing features is the addition of a half story under the eaves which was lighted by narrow horizontal windows within the architrave. This feature, together with the freely disposed plan was continued in the first mansard roof designs which follow. Of these the Rockefeller house is among the earliest (Figure 96). It has most of the features of the Kitchens house but now the added mansard roof permits a full third story. Each floor is also higher than in the older buildings. This typical residence was built in 1868 and was followed in turn by the fully formed "French" style in the early 1870's.

A characteristic such French design was built for O. D. Ford farther out on Euclid Avenue and was illustrated in the Atlas of 1874 (Figure 97). Here the vertical shapes of the windows and porch openings, the high tower and three floor plan together with the quoins and the decorated mansard roof all constitute the domestic counterpart for the official style which dominated the commercial and public buildings of the last years of this period.

The development of Cleveland in the first two decades of industrialization followed an inevitable course. The heritage of the mercantile period prescribed its direction. The mechanical rigidity of design which the industrial town inherited and the shortsightedness of accepted procedures foreordained the disintegration which took place. In these circumstances the railroads and heavy industry were as destructive of the physical health of the town as they were stimulating to its growth and economy. The complex results were far-reaching and in large measure decisive for the future: a confused and smoke-ridden industrial section, a crowded and ill-designed retail district, a gradually disintegrating residential area marked by extremes of protected luxury and incipient slums, an architecture which benefited immeasurably from the technical inventions but suffered the prevalent confusion in artistic form. By 1875 the city was already in the state of disorganization from which it has been suffering ever since. The boundaries of the original plan had been filled out and occupied, though hardly in the manner intended by the first surveyors. The area which today constitutes the central district of the city had been given its basic pattern and general character. The direction was charted for the subsequent changes in this district and whatever modifications were later made could be only in individual details.

The total form of the town at this time may be clearly visualized. Within the large triangular plot, some two miles wide at its greatest dimension and bounded by the lake, the river and Willson Avenue, the basic characteristics of the modern city were everywhere in evidence. On the flats from the mouth of the river to the outskirts of town on the south industry, wholesale houses and several railroad lines competed for space in the disorder which they themselves had created. The lake shore was bounded by the railroads interspersed with industry. Wholesale and retail firms vied with one another along the streets nearest the river mouth, and with rare exceptions the whole area near the Square was crowded by stores and office buildings. The Public Square itself was almost surrounded by com-

Figure 97. Ford House in 1876.

mercial structures and no longer had the character either of a park or of a civic center. Nowhere between Lake View Park and the city limits to east and south was there a plot of public ground outside the cemetery. With the exception of a few well protected avenues, the residential streets were lined by frame houses on narrow lots. The more pretentious architectural forms both public and residential presented a variety of styles resulting from the constantly changing fashions of these decades.

These conditions were the result of over three-quarters of a century of accumulation. Each period made its own contribution to this end result: the forms already on the ground became the foundation upon which new additions had to be made. At any given time there were these older physical obstacles to radical change. The street plan was fixed, the individual buildings inert, and the total form of the town inflexible. Expansion was easy so long as open ground was available on the edges of town, but once overbuilt, each area of the city could be modified only by the slow process of piecemeal replacement of parts.

In contrast to this lethargic and resistant character of the physical arrangements, the forces brought to bear upon the organism of the city were dynamic, expansive and volatile. At no time in the history of American cities to that period had such powerful influences been at work. The development of commerce and transportation, the geometric progression which marked the population figures, and the irresistible pressures of industrialization all focused upon the implanted and immobile forms of the city. Under the most favorable circumstances the difficulties inherent in this situation would have been nearly insoluble. To ameliorate in some measure the danger of disintegration thoughtful planning, great insight and vision, and sound principles upon which development could be based were all vitally necessary. None of these essentials was to be found in the history of Cleveland nor for that matter, of any American city in this period.

In recent decades the means to these ends have been gradually developed through building codes, zoning procedures and city-planning, but these were unheard of in the 19th century. In their absence the town was shaped inexorably by the forces and precepts of the time which were early established, became deeply entrenched, and were consistently effective throughout. These were conservativism and dependence upon tradition; improvisation rather than planning; and subservience to economic expediency. Together they produced the destructive results which marked the growth of the city before 1875.

These factors were at work when the town was founded in 1796 and continued to govern and shape its growth in the succeeding phases of development. The original plan was a traditional design: the surveyors came from New England and had every intention of reproducing an eastern village on the frontier. They applied the only plan they knew to the site, undeterred by the fact that the square checkerboard did not fit the triangular plot. They were forced to truncate the design and neglect the magnificent lakeside location to make it work, creating inflexibility and awkwardness with which the growing city had to deal for decades.

Nor did this plan foresee the future potential of the town. Moses Cleaveland was under instructions to find a site appropriate to a town which should become the capital city of a large hinterland, the Western Reserve itself. He chose a location on the lake at the mouth of a navigable river, clearly anticipating that the future city would become a port and market for the country around it. Yet the design which he laid out was one which was calculated for a small rural village: the Public Square was too small for a town of greater size and the central area too restricted; the mechanical regularity of the plan precluded the flexibility which the next decades of expansion would demand.

Conservatism and lack of foresight both compromised the utility of Cleveland's design at its very founding, but even more destructive results attended the economic policy which directed it. The original plan of the town, as of the Western Reserve as a whole, was calculated to promote sale of the land. The Connecticut Land Company had no other purpose than to ensure a generous return on an investment. The mechanical arrangement of the plan and the adjustment of lot sizes on the outskirts were calculated to encourage sales. Augustus Porter's suggestion that the lots around the Square and along the water front be reserved for public use was overridden. Thus the sole constructive idea of the time, dedicated to the public interest, was submerged by economic pressures.

Cleveland was born, so to speak, in bondage to these principles. In the ensuing decades the fetters were never cast aside. Conservatism dominated the expansion of the central area. When the increase of population made additional streets imperative, the traditional solution of further subdivision of the checkerboard was applied. This increased the number of available sites for building by the simplest and most obvious method, but thereby encouraged the density which was to overwhelm the central area within decades. Euclid Avenue and Prospect were, of course, exceptions to this prosaic thinking and well served the communications system at the center of town. The Baroque design of the projected Cleveland Centre in the flats also showed more imagination than was common, though economic forces destroyed it early in its career.

In architecture also development was retarded by a conservative tendency. The many phases of architectural fashion which originated elsewhere were adopted here, often somewhat tardily. But no significant innovation in structure or design may be credited to the builders of Cleveland, and no leading architect may be noted.

But conservatism was not the chief source of dislocation in the development of Cleveland. Lack of foresight and inability to anticipate the probable future needs of the community was still more disfiguring. It is true that the radical character of the changes and the speed with which they were effected after 1830 made anticipation of further needs forbiddingly difficult. The revolutionary scope and the acceleration of mercantile expansion and industrialization would have defied the powers of a seer. Nonetheless, in Cleveland, there is little evidence of any long-range planning at all. Each new problem from the simplest to the most complex seems to have been met by improvisation.

The policy applied to land use is the most flagrant example of shortsightedness. Before many decades had passed the growth of the town had created a need for parks and public grounds. In retrospect it is clear that the adamant refusal of the city council to entertain the repeated petitions and its rejection of proferred land were disastrous oversights. The city was to pay dearly, in the aftermath, in the lack of open space and recreation areas. This same inability to anticipate the needs of a growing community doomed the Public Square to commercial uses and destroyed its potentialities as a civic center. Meantime the finest sites for recreational facilities were engulfed by commerce and then by the railroads and industry. In the absence of reservations for public use the entire waterfront on both lake shore and river bank were taken over. The one attempt to cultivate these natural advantages by the development of Lake View Park was entirely inadequate and since the park had to compete with neighboring railroads and industry, it was never very satisfactory as a recreation area.

In the absence of any controlling design the areas of specialization in the city grew and developed in disorder, one improvised step at a time. As early as 1833 when Whelpley recorded the appearance of various parts of town, Superior Street was already lined by closely-spaced stores and the river banks had begun their disorderly career. The small population was still easily accommodated on generous lots at this time though the dangers of mechanical regularity were even then present in the residential districts. In the next twenty years these incipient characteristics of each section of town were, through the almost complete absence of planning, to become imbedded in confusion and congestion. Only on a few well protected residential streets were the cumulative forces of expansion held sufficiently in check to preserve order for a few years.

Lack of planning and the policy of improvization not only permitted disorder and congestion, it countenanced wholesale destruction of established values. The older residential districts suffered most on this score. Since the needs of commerce had not been anticipated and no proper space alloted to its expansion, it had no choice but to encroach upon residential streets and the periphery of the Public Square. By a gradual but steady process of attrition the northwest quadrant of the city was destroyed for residential purposes, the Square eliminated as a civic center, and the invasion of the eastern approaches of the city commenced.

The failure to provide proper space for commercial development, and to prevent the disintegration of established forms was serious in the mercantile period. It became disastrous under industrial expansion. Given full freedom to locate according to their own convenience, the railroads and heavy industry drove southward from the lake to occupy the entire river bed, pushed the wholesale and warehouse buildings out of the flats, and cross-hatched the town with road beds and factories. No amount of forethought could have prevented all the ills attendant upon such rapid change and such powerful forces as those of this period, but the blunders of improvisation greatly increased their destructive capacities.

Mere absence of planning permitted many abuses and lack of foresight alone was therefore a serious matter. Its effects, however, were doubled by the economic policies of the period. Cleveland grew up with the development of the system of laissez-faire, and in the final analysis this view was the most destructive element in the formation of the city.

Economic interests repeatedly succeeded in thwarting the few efforts made to preserve the best interests of the city. Real estate speculation was encouraged by the conditions of rapid expansion and the design of whole areas of town was permitted to pass into the hands of these operators. The disorder of the flats and the crowding of the retail districts were allowed because these were the sources of prosperity and the evidence of economic progress. The mechanical expansion of the street plan was adopted because this system provided a larger number of valuable sites and promoted sales.

In the industrial period the economic forces reigned supreme. Prosperity of the railroads and of industry and trade was the motivating force which permitted indiscriminate choice of rights-of-way and of industrial sites, which prevented the control of smoke and allowed pollution of the waters. Economic interests successfully thwarted the few efforts made to establish controls over these destructive practices, a campaign to which the newspapers shortsightedly lent their active support.

In retrospect it seems the bitterest irony that during these decades of energetic growth and youthful exuberance, the forces of conservatism, improvisation and economic expediency should have been permitted to exert their baleful influence. The damage, however, was now done and in the aftermath its full destructive effect was finally realized.

CHAPTER FIVE

EPILOGUE: CLEVELAND AFTER 1875

The adolescence of Cleveland as an urban complex was now over, and the story of its maturity lies outside the scope of this study. Nonetheless, it may be well to note the aftermath in the adult city. As with a living organism, so with the city, the forms and the practices of its youth continue to shape and direct its maturity. After 1875 the town as first designed became, one step at a time, the center of a vast metropolitan area. This central city was rapidly aging, the symptoms of debilitation were already well advanced as its vitality seeped away to the growing suburbs. Not until comparatively recent years has a concerted effort been made to reverse this degenerative trend.

Meantime the way which had been charted before 1875 was pursued without substantial change for another several decades. While the pace of development still further accelerated and the problems increased, the correctives remained undiscovered. After the Civil War, and in part due to its stimulation, the cities of the north (and especially Cleveland) witnessed a new and unprecedented expansion of industrial capacity. Many of the steel plants which are still the key industries of the city today were founded in the 1880's. Innumerable lesser industries followed, crowding the lakefront and the Cuyahoga Valley, and stretching along the lines of the railroads. As early as the 1870's a comprehensive industrial site was laid out between St. Clair and the lake

from East 25th Street to East 55th. By 1890 the frontiers of industrial Cleveland could be defined as the area between East 105th Street and West 65th, pre-empting the entire lake frontage. The occupation by industry of the Cuyahoga Valley, already well advanced, was virtually completed by the 1920's when nearly 400 acres of remaining swamp land were filled and reclaimed for steel plants. A new wave of railroad building, including spur lines to supply industry, spread these effects more densely across the city.

When the capacity of the center of town to accommodate industry was reached, the new suburban areas were invaded. As usual the rail-lines controlled their location and belts of manufacturing extended east, south and west carrying the familiar smoke and debris into new residential communities.

Wholesale firms and warehouses followed in the wake of manufacturing. They too were served by the railroads and the competition for space along the rights of way became intense, always at the expense of the livability of the town. As before, retail firms and residences were replaced by industry and warehouses wherever economic expediency dictated.

As the population density increased, retail firms kept pace and, as usual, their depredations upon residential areas were uncontrolled. By a continuing process the main avenues radi-

151

ating from the Public Square, all at one time flanked by the finest homes in the city, succumbed to this onslaught. Illustrious Euclid Avenue, long protected by the prestige and influence of its property-owners, is at present an unbroken stretch of commercial buildings or forlorn remnants of once fine houses long since remodelled for commercial use. The side streets have followed the same trend until the deterioration of residential values was virtually complete in the area of the original city. With no adequate protection against these disintegrative forces, the remaining patches of houses degenerated rapidly. They were occupied by the low income groups which could not escape to better suburban communities. Return to the landlords diminished, crowding increased, maintenance was neglected and the vicious circle was completed only when slums remained.

New technology of construction contributed materially to this transformation of the center of the city. The replacement of obsolete buildings by higher structures was under way before 1875, but thereafter the steel frame and reinforced concrete permitted and encouraged even higher buildings. As population increased and land values soared, each square foot had to accommodate more people and provide a higher return on investment. The skyscraper was the obvious solution. Office buildings and hotels, stores and warehouses, rose in intensive competition for the available footage. As no space had been provided between earlier buildings, so now their soaring replacements crowded the downtown area, ruthlessly competing with one another for sunlight and air. The streets of the original village plan now lay prostrate at the bottom of high, slab-sided cliffs of buildings in unbroken array virtually throughout the downtown area.

Meantime railroad and industrial expansion was still further increasing the twin nuisances of air and water pollution. By the 1880's they had reached the proportions of a blight at the center of town: a blight which spread with the extension of railroads and manufacturing. In 1883 legislative power to control smoke was granted the city, but as in earlier times, the efforts to curb industry were ineffective. Accounts of the 1890's note that no appreciable abatement of the nuisance could then be detected. Similarly the pollution of the river and lake increased each year as a larger volume of industrial waste was added to the discharge of the sewers. In 1881 the Health Department lodged formal protests against these practices and these too were largely disregarded. Throughout the last decades of the 19th century the decay of the central city was hastened and the flight to the suburbs encouraged by these practices.

The principal deterrent to a mass exodus to escape these increasingly adverse conditions was the inadequate transportation. One step at a time, however, technology provided the means to this end. In 1884 the first electrified street railroad designed for public use appeared. A brief experiment with cable cars on Superior and Payne Avenues was abandoned but by 1893 street car lines had been so extended that consolidation into two companies became necessary. In the next years inter-urban lines connected Cleveland to its growing suburbs and even to distant towns. These lines now made it possible to live at a distance from the debris and smoke of the center of town and still benefit from its industrial and commercial progress. Thus further extension of the city boundaries was encouraged and new suburban communities were made possible. Rapid transit lines, beginning with the Shaker Rapid in the 1920's, and since multiplied, increased the capacity and speed of public conveyances.

The most revolutionary change in transportation, however, was produced by the development of the internal combustion engine. The truck, the automobile, and the bus created revolutionary changes in the urban communities throughout the United States. And since none of these major changes could have been anticipated and provided for, the dislocations which ensued were far-reaching. Added to the already serious deterioration of the city they served to complete the degeneration of the central area.

The mobility provided by the private automobile and the public bus encouraged the development of suburban communities on a grand scale. In the more than fifty satellite towns which now surround Cleveland proper, a large proportion of the population is employed in the central city. Progressively as the decades passed, the streets of Cleveland were called upon to carry a burden of commuter vehicles for which they had never been intended. The checkerboard of narrow streets with crossings at short intervals frustrated the potentialities of the motor-car and created unforeseen hazards for the pedestrian. The major avenues converging upon the Public Square which once served so well to aid the expansion of the town and lead to neighboring villages, now served to funnel an overwhelming current of vehicles upon the virtual dead-end of the Public Square. The result was blockade rather than mobility.

Trucking on an increasing scale encouraged a further dissemination of industry and commerce throughout the downtown area. Once largely dependent upon the railroads, manufacturing and commerce could now be supplied by trucks. Thus the few remaining residential areas were invaded and exhaust fumes added materially to the air pollution provided by railroad and industry. Finally, the disposition of these vehicles once they had reached the downtown area became yearly a more acute problem which has not yet been completely solved.

In retrospect it is difficult to understand why it was necessary to wait until the condition of the city was desperate before the first concerted efforts were made to find corrections for the worst abuses. However, at the turn of the century a beginning was finally made. The struggle was severe and the processes slow and costly. Old habits and methods had to be changed, new means determined upon and executed in the face of organized opposition and the pleading of special interests. Legal precedent had to be established and tested by litigation in a long, involved and often ill-tempered process before improvements could be effected. The end has by no means been reached, but sufficient progress has already been made so that the growth of the city is no longer guided exclusively by expediency and economic self-interest.

In general the improvements instituted in the last 70 odd years fall into one of two categories: better methods and controls to direct development; and the reclamation of old and the building of new structures in the city. The Cleveland Chapter of the American Institute of Architects was established in 1887, dedicated then as it is now to the improvement of architectural practice and the maintenance of high professional standards. Though difficult to measure, this acknowledged leadership has undoubtedly affected the quality of Cleveland architecture over the decades. In 1888 a Department of Buildings was instituted in the city to grant permits for construction and thus regularize the industry. This was followed by the first Building Code in 1905 which had the effect, as intended, to establish and enforce standards in the quality of materials and structure. A Builders' Exchange, founded in 1890, and the Cleveland Real Estate Board in 1892, both sought the improvement of conditions in construction and marketing. In the same year the Park Act created the Board of Park Commissioners which has been instrumental in developing an excellent park system especially on the outskirts of Greater Cleveland.

As early as 1892 the demand arose for a more authoritative and professional body to guide the growth of the city. It was only in 1913, however, that the City Planning Commission was finally chartered. At first it was concerned primarily with the development of the Mall in downtown Cleveland, with plans for new streets and with control of the form of the new skyscrapers by set-back regulations.

Since this modest beginning the commission has gradually expanded its sphere of authority until at the present time virtually all plans and designs for the physical development of the city come within its purview. Meantime zoning codes were adopted which sought to preserve the character and integrity of the specialized areas of the city and prevent that wholesale destruction of residential districts which earlier decades had countenanced.

By these several means a measure of control over the development of the city has been achieved. Standards have been set, the worst abuses curbed, and civic interests served.

Meantime some of the degeneration of the central city has been alleviated by replacement of obsolete structures and by new construction. As early as 1893, inspired by the grandeur of the World's Columbian Exposition in Chicago. the design of a monumental center for Cleveland was demanded. Implementation began in 1900 and continued over the next decades. Though incomplete on the west side, a spacious center of municipal buildings axially grouped around an open Mall now serves as a focus of civic functions in Cleveland. This so-called Group Plan has thus reestablished the physical and symbolic center which was lost when the Public Square was given over to commerce in earlier decades.

In 1915 the Terminal Group, dominated by the Terminal Tower and including a hotel, department store, banks and a central Post Office, was conceived. Delayed by World War I, this enormous project was implemented in the 1920's. It occupied that awkward triangular plot southwest of the Square, which was part of the original design, obliterating many streets and deteriorated commercial buildings and creating the city's highest skyscraper above a centrally located railroad terminal.

Adjacent to the Mall on the east, two large areas of downtown Cleveland have been chosen for major renewal projects, designated Erieview I and II. The first is now under way and the second in the planning stage. These, together with several less extensive projects, envision a total redesign of a major part of the center of the city: clearing obsolete buildings and providing a balanced design of office buildings, stores, hotels, apartments, open-space and pedestrian malls. A major surgical operation on the degenerated downtown area is involved with a view to rehabilitation and balanced design.

The traffic problems at the center have been vigorously attacked, although the entrenched real-estate values along their flanks of course have made the widening of streets in this area virtually impossible. One-way traffic, the removal of street cars in favor of buses and the elaborate system of traffic controls by lanes and signals have alleviated the situation to some degree, but the most effective remedy has been a whole new system of arterial boulevards supplemented by high level bridges to span the river. Freeways along the lakeshore on filled land, and radiating outward from the center of town, all interconnected by belts which circumnavigate the center, have served to move cars more efficiently. Thus major incisions in the old center have been necessary to adapt it to the unanticipated demands of surface transportation. Since the destination of much of this traffic is the center of town, innumerable parking lots and garages have been constructed, and each new building is now required to provide parking space for its tenants within the building itself.

Since the 1930's various means have been developed to restore the remaining residential areas in downtown Cleveland. Total clearance and mass housing were applied to the worst slums. These provided more durable structures, community centers and open space for the low income groups which remained in the area. Rehabilitation by the owners of houses less completely deteriorated has been encouraged with partial success. Wherever possible small play areas have been opened up to relieve the congestion of these overcrowded sections. Although no major park or recreation area has yet been developed downtown, the band of filled land along the lake is occupied by a parking lot, an airport and the stadium in addition to the freeway. Nevertheless, in a continuing program of reclamation and rebuilding some improvement may be seen in this once slum-ridden section of the city.

Meantime, after almost a century of abortive effort, progress has recently been made in the control of air pollution. More stringent and enforceable laws aided by a new sense of public responsibility on the part of industry, has in the last few years reduced smoke and debris. The improvement in the liveability of the downtown area has been marked. The river and the lake, however, are still so badly polluted as to be a serious health hazard. Thus is Cleveland denied the proper use of one of its finest resources.

In the last 60-odd years, then, the means to a partial rehabilitation of the old, original city have been sought out and implemented. It is unfortunately true that the salutary effects of this concerted and continuing effort have been repeatedly curbed and frustrated. The ingenuity of private interests has found ways to evade zoning regulations, and circumvent building codes. The City Planning Commission has to engage in an unending struggle against special and often contradictory interests to prevent frustration of its plans. The traffic problem is hardly diminished despite all the means employed as the number of cars increases and suburban areas are extended. Artificially inflated land values and the faceless monotony of new buildings, dictated by soaring costs and ruthless speculation, largely vitiate the efforts to improve the character of the city. Most destructive of all, the ubiquitous advertising signs and neon lights which reduce the central city to an artistic jungle remain, undirected and uncontrolled.

Despite these deterrents, the progress which has been made in this century, and especially within the last decade against continuing opposition and problems of enormous complexity is impressive. The end is not yet in sight, and the cost in labor and expense will be enormous, but at least, for the first time in its history, the city of Cleveland is actively and systematically engaged in finding the means to control its physical destiny.

FOOTNOTES TO THE TEXT

The original street names will be used in this study to maintain consistency; but to assist the present-day reader, the designation of streets adopted in 1906 will appear in parenthesis at the first mention.

[1] This definition is quoted by Orth, S. P., *History of Cleveland.* Chicago, Clarke, 1910, 38.

[2] The history of these surveys is recorded by Baker, Samuel J., "The Original Surveys of Cleveland," *Journal of the Association of Engineering Societies,* III, no. 10 (August, 1884), 218.

[3] See Williams, Arthur B., *Geology of the Cleveland Region.* Cleveland, Museum of Natural History, 1940.

[4] In 1801 Spafford had added Superior Lane as an extension of Superior Street, thus bringing again to four the number of connections between the town and the river. This last, however, was on a very steep grade until regraded at a later date. George Merwin, *Annals of the Early Settler's Association,* I. no. 5, 19, says: "About the year 1830 Superior Street was graded from the west line of Bank to the river, the cutting at the Atwater building the end of Superior Street at its juncture with Superior Lane was twenty-one feet . . ."

[5] As an instance, James D. Campbell describes his recollections of Cleveland when he arrived in 1835 in these terms: "With its splendid houses, its numerous groves, its lofty outlook on the lake, its clear atmosphere as yet unpolluted by smoke, Cleveland was as beautiful a village as could be found west of New Haven." (*Cleveland Leader.* February 2, 1896.)

[6] Whittlesey, Charles, "Origin of the American System of Land Survey," *Journal of the Association of Engineering Societies,* III, no. 10 (August, 1884), 275-280 discusses the reasons for the popularity of this method of survey.

[7] Johnson, Crisfield, *History of Cuyahoga County.* Philadelphia, Ensign, 1879, records the following stipulations by Porter: to reserve the

156

lots surrounding the Public Square for public purposes and such portions of the flats as considered advisable; to sell every fourth lot to anyone who promised to settle in 1797 and permit him to purchase one town lot for $50, one ten-acre lot for $2 per acre, and one hundred-acre lot for $1.50 per acre. Town lots were to be paid for in cash, the others by a down payment of 20% and the remainder in three annual installments.

[8] In a letter to John Bar, dated December 1858, now *Mss #166* in the Western Reserve Historical Society, Alfred Kelley described conditions in early Cleveland. On page 14 this paragraph, indicative of the situation, is included: "The construction of the turnpike road (after the War of 1812) from Cleveland to Wooster and a more direct and better road into the central part of the state, and of a free turnpike to Wellsville opened new, though imperfect channels of trade which gave to the prosperity of Cleveland a decided impetus. They first opened a communication between the Lake, at Cleveland and several of the best settled and most productive counties within the Northern half of Ohio that had previously been tributary to other ports. The latter connected the Lake and Ohio river at the points of their nearest approach to each other."

[9] These figures are from Whittlesey, *Early History of Cleveland, Ohio.* Cleveland, Fairbanks, Benedict, 1867, 456.

[10] John Bar, "Cleveland, Ohio — Western Reserve, etc." *National Magazine,* II, no. 7 (December, 1845), 599-623, states in part: "From 1800 to 1812, the populative receipts (in Cleveland) were few and far between: the town waxed not in importance, although the country, stretching away from it, was filling up with a class of yeomanry of worth and industry . . ." Benton, Elbert Jay, *Cultural Story of an American City, Cleveland,* 1943, I, 44, publishes the population of Cleveland compared to the neighboring towns to the east in 1820. Every one of these towns had a larger population than Cleveland at that date.

[11] See Kennedy, James Harrison, *A History of the City of Cleveland*. Cleveland, Imperial, 1896, 173.

[12] This group was organized in 1880 and its membership consisted of those who were early pioneers in Cleveland. At its annual meetings talks were given and papers read pertaining to the events of Cleveland's early years. These constitute an invaluable record of the first decades of the town's existence, although they are to be used as authentic source material with due caution as they are the reminiscences of elderly people some fifty to seventy years after the events described.

[13] Morgan I. A., "A sketch of pioneer life," *Annals of the Early Settler's Association*. II, no. 11, 407.

[14] Williamson, S., "Reminiscences," *Annals of the Early Settler's Association*. I, no. 1, 54-56. The Bank Street twice referred to in this passage is in error. Bank runs parallel to Water Street and does not intersect it as indicated. The elderly Mr. Williamson confused Bank with Lake Street, for Kelley's house is recorded in Whittlesey, *Early History, etc.*, as being on the corner of Water and Lake.

[15] Morgan, I. A., "What I recollect," *Annals of the Early Settler's Association*. II. no. 2, appendix, 65.

[16] Johnson, *op. cit.*, 226 describes such cabins on the Western Reserve. Similar cabins are still to be found in the backwoods of eastern Canada where conditions approximate those of a pioneer situation. In remote sections, accessible only by canoe, no sawn lumber is used. Even floors and roofs are of small poles, those in the floor slightly flattened with the broad-axe to provide a more level surface. Doors and windows of glass are usually provided since these can be brought in by canoe and carried across the portages. Iron stoves, also transportable, are used for heat.

[17] Because of its appearance some authorities have erroneously considered this the first frame house in Cleveland. Johnson, *op. cit.*, 231, fell into this error.

[18] Orth, *op. cit.*, 100. See also Johnson, *op. cit.*, 231.

[19] Benton, *op. cit.*, I, 10 ff. and Kennedy, *op. cit.*, 140.

[20] Orth, *op. cit.*, 612. This store is mentioned, though not described, by Kelley in the letter quoted in the next paragraph.

[21] Orth, *loc. cit.*

[22] Letter to John Bar, *Mss #166*. Western Reserve Historical Society.

[23] Watkins, George, "Early Days," *Annals of the Early Settler's Association*, II, no. 7, 20. Such buildings could be erected more quickly and easily when power saws became available. The first in the immediate vicinity of Cleveland was apparently that set up by Kingsbury on Mill Creek in 1800. Others soon followed and the cutting of boards and small timbers was thereby facilitated.

[24] Avery, Elroy McKendree, *A History of Cleveland and Its Environs*. Chicago, Lewis, 1918. This authority gives a list of the extraordinary attainments of Levi Johnson on page 93 of volume I.

[25] All recent authorities agree on the principal features of this building as here described. However, Avery, *op. cit.*, states that the building had an inside staircase on the landing of which there was a fireplace. Benton, *op. cit.*, I, 11 mentions a woodstove for heat. Orth, *op. cit.*, 266 insists on an outside staircase. On the other hand the accounts in the *Annals of the Early Settler's Association* several times refer to the "log court house". I. A. Morgan, who knew the building intimately states with great certainty (*Annals, etc.*, II, no. 2, appendix, 64): "It has been said that the first court house was built of logs. This is a mistake. It was a frame, except the jail room on the lower floor, which was constructed of logs notched together and sided up like the other parts of the building." With this description Whittlesey, *Early History etc.*, 473, agrees, and he further characterizes the jail as being "constructed of blocks of square timber three feet long, placed endwise and bolted together."

[26] See Avery, *op. cit.*, 125.

[27] See Peattie, Roderick, *Geography of Ohio*. Geological Survey of Ohio, fourth series, Bulletin 27, Columbus, 1923.

[28] A detailed account of these operations is given by Griswold, Seneca O., "The corporate birth and growth of Cleveland," *Western Reserve and Northern Ohio Historical Society. Tract no. 62.* (July 22, 1884) 302.

[29] See Griswold, *op. cit.*, *passim*.

[30] The map of annexations in the Cleveland Engineer's office, a reduced facsimile of which was published by Orth, *op. cit.*, 46, shows the outlines of the village as defined on December 23, 1814. This map is the authoritative document of the city boundaries at various dates and will be again referred to in this paper.

[31] Griswold, *op. cit.*, does not include Bond in the list of streets surveyed in 1815. Orth, *op. cit.*, 51, does so include it. Logic would tend to support Orth inasmuch as Bond Street is essential to the symmetry of the arrangement, and it has been noted that regularity was a paramount consideration in the design of the streets of Cleveland in this period. The street designations in parentheses are those of the present day; a wholesale relabelling of streets was done in 1906.

[32] The name "Federal" was discarded about 1820 in favor of St. Clair in honor of the first governor of the Territory. See Orth, *op. cit.*, 52. the name St. Clair will therefore be used hereafter in this account. Similarly the spelling of Cleveland was changed by omission of the "a" in this period, although the old spelling occurs occasionally until about 1835.

[33] See Griswold. *op. cit.*, 302.

[34] Watkins, George, *op. cit.*, 18.

[35]Rice, Harvey, *Annals of the Early Settler's Association*. III, no. 1, 35.

[36]*Annals of the Early Settler's Association*, I, no. 2, appendix, 76.

[37]The first directory for Cleveland published in 1837 (McCabe, Julius P. Bolivar, *Directory. Cleveland and Ohio City, for the years 1837-1838*. Cleveland, Sanford and Lott, 1837, 45) lists forty-nine carpenters, twenty-nine masons and nineteen painters. In 1837 the population of Cleveland was 5000 persons. If the proportions of artisans to population was relatively constant, 1830 should have seen some ten carpenters, six masons and four painters at that time.

[38]*Annals of the Early Settler's Association*, I, no. 2, appendix, 64.

[39]McCabe, *op. cit.*

[40]*Annals of the Early Settler's Association*, I, no. 5, 19. The church was actually destroyed on March 30, 1854.

[41]*Trinity Cathedral Guide*, Cleveland, 1912, 17.

[42]McCabe, *op. cit.*, 43.

[43]*Past and Present of Grace Church*. Cleveland, Williams, 1898. Chapter by H. E. Henderson, *The History of Grace Church*.

[44]See Peattie, *op. cit.*, 97 ff., for a history of canal development in Ohio.

[45]See Orth, *op. cit.*, table on page 701.

[46]Orth, *op cit.*, compiled numerous statistics on lake traffic in chapter LXX.

[47]Table, Whittlesey, *Early History*, 456.

[48]Knight and Parson's, *Business Directory of the City of Cleveland*, Cleveland, 1853, 17.

[49]See Orth, *op cit.*, 45 ff., and Griswold, *op. cit.*, 47.

[50]McCabe, *op. cit.*, 46 describes Clinton Park in these terms: ". . . situated half a mile from the court house, on the bank of Lake Erie — which although a wilderness of unsightly stumps and girdled trees two years ago [1835], is already encircled with some suburban villas embosomed in gardens of the most picturesque beauty. The Park itself is about thirty rods in length and occupies the space between Wilson Street and Lake Street." Despite this auspicious start the panic of 1837 almost destroyed the accomplishments of its early residents. See Orth, *op. cit.*, 47.

[51]Howe, Henry, *Historical Collections of Ohio*. Cincinnati, Bradley, 1849.

[52]Mss. 2541. Western Reserve Historical Society.

[53]See Orth, *op. cit.*, 60 f.

[54]Curiously enough, in view of the large quantities of brick which were obviously required by the popularity of this material in the canal period, the records pertaining to this industry are sparse. It is probable that individual brickyards were small concerns with an investment and output insufficient to warrant mention as industries. In any case no directory before that of 1857 lists brickmakers among the occupations and industries of Cleveland. At that time three concerns are identified in the directory and the number noted increases in subsequent years. The first notice of the industry is that found in the Federal Census of 1840 which gives these figures for the city of Cleveland: invested in manufacture of brick and lime, $12,500; men employed, 26; product valued at $8,540. In 1860 the same source states: invested $12,450; establishments 8; employed 88; value of product $42,650. In the *Annual Statement of the Trade, Commerce and Manufactures of the City of Cleveland for the Year 1865* (Cleveland, Fairbanks, Benedict, 1866, p. 22) this short paragraph is devoted to the industry: "There are some dozen brickyards in the immediate vicinity of Cleveland. The amount of brick made in 1865 was about seven millions, at an average value of six dollars per thousand. The Cleveland brick are in good repute and are sent abroad in large quantities."

[55]A valuable reference list of these publications together with the American libraries in which they may be found in Hitchcock, Henry Russell, *American Architectural Books*. Minneapolis, University of Minnesota press, 1946.

[56]The photograph from which this illustration is taken is in the Cleveland Public Library where it is wrongly labelled. There it is dated 1900 and described as the wrecking of the hotel to make way for the Rockefeller Building. Study of the remaining exterior wall and the printing of the name over the columns to the left clearly reveals that these features are quite different from the appearance of the house after the remodelling of the 1880's and accord exactly with its appearance before that remodelling The photograph was therefore taken during this remodelling which was the only time in the history of the building when such an extensive change as is here depicted was undertaken.

[57]See Freese, *op. cit.*, 19 f.

[58]The historian of Presbyterianism in Cleveland is: Ludlow, A. C., *The Old Stone Church*. Privately printed, 1920, and Ludlow, A. C., and Mrs. A. C., *History of Cleveland Presbyterianism*. Cleveland, Bayne, 1896. See also the *Annals of the First Presbyterian Church of Cleveland*, 1820-1895. Cleveland, Winn and Judson, 1895, 192-213.

[59]See Houck, George Francis, *The Church in Northern Ohio and in the Diocese of Cleveland, from 1817 to Sept. 1887*. New York, Benziger, 1887, 200-28. Also Houck, G. F., *History of Catholicity in Northern Ohio*. Cleveland, Savage, 1903, 64 ff. and 195-98.

[60]Smead and Cowles, *General Business Directory for the City of Cleveland, Compiled by I. N. Mason*, Cleveland, 1850, 43.

[61]Knight and Parson's, *op., cit.*, 56-57. See also Pomeroy, Charles S., *An Historical Sketch Reviewing the Origin and Growth of the*

Second Presbyterian Church, Cleveland, Ohio. Cleveland, Leader, 1876.

[62]See, Upjohn, Everard, *Richard Upjohn, Architect and Churchman,* New York Columbia, 1939, Appendix, Class A, p. 200.

[63]A concise account of the railroads which entered Cleveland and the details of their complex early history are given in Orth, *op. cit.,* 730-44, and in Peattie, *op. cit.,* 105 ff.

[64]No exact figures are available on the population west of the river when the two towns were joined in 1854. The only figures before the union are those for 1850 when Ohio City had approximately 4000 inhabitants. Of the 43,838 population in 1860 an estimated 8000 lived west of the river. For the purposes of this study the physical development of the west side of the river will not be considered since it in no pertinent way effects the central problem of this study. The two sections of town, incidentally, continued to develop along separate lines despite their political association after 1854. This independence is still to be noted in Cleveland today, the rivalry on opposite sides of the river being almost unabated even now.

[65]See Orth, *op. cit.,* Chapter VI, passim.

[66]See Orth, *op. cit.,* Chapter XII, passim.

[67]See Orth, *op. cit.,* 62 ff.

[68]See Payne, *op. cit.,* 52 ff.

[69]Boyd, Andrew, *Cleveland Directory,* 1863-64. Cleveland, Fairbanks and Benedict, 1863, 95.

[70]Payne, *op. cit.,* 69.

[71]As instances of such remodelling, these two notices may be quoted: "The Tuttle store on Superior St. is undergoing some changes and improvements. The front is to be changed to one with iron columns." (*Leader,* August 15, 1856) and, "A handsome portico is being erected over the Bank St. entrance to the Weddell House, the supporting pillars being of cast iron." (*Leader,* January 30, 1863).

[72]*Cleveland Leader,* May 3 and July 10, 1858 respectively.

[73]Fairbairn, William, *On the Application of Cast and Wrought Iron to Building Purposes.* New York, Wiley, 1854. The fact of the publication of this volume in this country though the author was an Englishman indicates the interest in these structural problems here and greatly speeded the dissemination of the engineering knowledge requisite to erecting such structures.

[74]Quotation from the *Leader,* October 26, 1857.

[75]*Cleveland Leader,* June 4 and December 30, 1858, respectively.

[76]Such formal training, in fact, became available for the first time in this period. The American Institute of Architects was founded in 1857, the first school of architecture at M. I. T. in 1866. See Fitch, James Marston, *American Building.* Boston, Houghton, Mifflin, 1948, 101. The earliest notice of the arrival in Cleveland of an architect with such a background is the following: "Joseph Ireland, architect, an associate member of the American Institute of Architects and a former pupil of R. G. Hatfield esq., will open an office at 225 Superior St. and there will conduct his business, on and after Jan. 25, 1865." (*Leader,* January 6, 1865).

[77]In the *Leader* on November 2, 1858, p. 3, col. 2 this notice was published: "A large number of new buildings are in process of erection in different parts of the city. A greater part of these are small and of wood, ranging in value from $200 to $500. There are, however, quite a respectable number of good and substantial dwellings going up."

[78]*Op. cit.,* 46.

[79]Payne, *op. cit.,* 172 is the authority for this date of completion.

[80]*Op. cit.,* 79 f. More detailed accounts of the building activities of the school board are given in Akers, William Joseph, *Cleveland Public Schools in the Nineteenth Century.* Cleveland, Bayre, 1901, passim, and in the annual reports of the school board. The information on the public schools on these pages is taken from these sources and from Freese, *op. cit.*

[81]The *Leader* on June 27, 1855, p. 3, col. 2; "We take pleasure in announcing that another model school house was completed last week in this city. We refer to the one on Eagle St. The building is of brick; and is substantially as well as elegantly furnished on the inside. The builders were Messrs. Kidney, Blair; Hurd and Porter, architects." Heard seems to have had some sort of an arrangement with the school board after 1855, for almost all the subsequent designs in this period were by him, either with Porter or with his later partner, Blythe.

[82]The authority for this date is the *Leader* on May 31, 1865, p. 4, col. 3: "The Brownell St. school house building which was commenced last August will be completed in September. The cost is between $35,000 and $40,000. It is 108 by 76 feet, and is three stories high. The structure has a tin and slate roof." Akers, *op. cit.,* also gives 1865 as the date of the opening of this school. As the 1868 design of the St. Clair Street school replaced this one only three years later, the Brownell school was a unique building.

[83]The cost and name of the architect appeared in the *Daily True Democrat* for April 23, 1853.

[84]*Op. cit.,* 138 f.

[85]See Ludlow, A. C., *Old Stone Church,* 129 ff.

[86]*Op. cit.,* 145 f.

[87]*Op. cit.,* 149-152 is the source for the three quotations which follow.

BIBLIOGRAPHY

PART I   *History of Ohio*

Hatcher, Harlan, *The Buckeye Country*. New York, Kinsey, 1940.

Hatcher, Harlan, *Lake Erie*. New York, Bobbs-Merrill, 1944.

Hinsdale, Burke Aaron, *The Old Northwest*. New York, MacCoun, 1888.

Howe, Henry, *Historical Collections of Ohio*. Cincinnati, Bradley, 1849.

McClelland, C. R., and Huntington, C. C., *History of the Ohio Canal*. Columbus, Heer, 1905.

Peattie, Roderick, *Geography of Ohio*. Geological Survey of Ohio, Fourth Series, Bulletin 27, Columbus, 1923.

Roseboom, Eugene H., and Weisenberger, Francis P., *History of Ohio*. Columbus, 1942.

Utter, William T., *The Frontier State*. Columbus, 1942.

Wright, George F., *The Ice Age in North America*. New York, Appleton, 1889.

PART II   *History of the Western Reserve*

Bar, John, "Cleveland, Ohio-Western Reserve, etc.," *Fisher's National Magazine*, II, no. 7 (December, 1845), 599-623.

Brainard, E. P., "Western Reserve," *Magazine of Western History*, II, 343.

Carpenter, Helen M., "The Origin and Location of the Firelands of the Western Reserve," *Ohio State Archaeological and Historical Quarterly*, XLIV (1935), 163-203.

Cherry, P. P., *The Western Reserve and Early Ohio*. Akron, Fouse, 1921.

Hatcher, Harlan, *The Western Reserve*. Indianapolis, Bobbs-Merrill, 1949.

Mills, William Stowell, *The Story of the Western Reserve of Connecticut*. New York, Brown and Wilson, 1900.

Pease, Seth, "Journals of Seth Pease to and from New Connecticut, 1796-98," *Western Reserve Historical Society, Tract no. 94*, (1914), 27-132.

Rice, Harvey, *Pioneers of the Western Reserve*. Boston, Lee and Shepard, 1883.

Rice, Harvey, *Sketches of Western Life*. Boston, Lee and Shepard, 1887.

Upton, Harriet Taylor, *History of the Western Reserve*. New York, Lewis, 1910.

Waite, Frederick Clayton, "The Derivation and Significance of the Term Western Reserve," *Western Reserve University Bulletin* XXVIII, no. 8 (1923).

Whittlesey, Charles, "Origin of the American System of Land Surveys," *Journal of the Association of Engineering Societies*, III, no. 10 (August, 1884), 275-280.

Whittlesey, Charles, "Western Reserve — Origin of Title," *Western Reserve and Northern Ohio Historical Society. Tract no. 33*, (1876).

Whittlesey, Charles, "Western Reserve Surveys," *Annals of the Early Settler's Association*, I, no. 4, 69-78, Cleveland, 1883.

PART III   *History of Cuyahoga County*

Coates, William R., *A History of Cuyahoga County and the City of Cleveland*. Chicago, American Historical Society, 1924.

Johnson, Crisfield, *History of Cuyahoga County*. Philadelphia, Ensign, 1879.

PART IV   *History of the City of Cleveland*

A Chronology of the City of Cleveland from 1796. Compiled by the history division of the Cleveland Public Library (type-written manuscript), 1936.

160

Annals of Cleveland, 1818-. A Digest and Index of Newspaper Record of Events and Opinions. W. P. A., 1937-June 1939.

Annual Statement of the Trade, Commerce and Manufactures of the City of Cleveland for the year 1865. Cleveland, Fairbanks, Benedict, 1866.

Avery, Elroy McKendree, *A History of Cleveland and Its Environs.* 3 vol. Chicago, Lewis, 1918.

Benton, Elbert Jay, *Cultural Story of an American City. Cleveland.* 3 parts. Western Reserve Historical Society, 1943-46.

"The History of Cleveland," *The Traveller*, New York, December 25, 1858.

Kelley, Alfred, *Letter to John Bar. Mss #166.* Western Reserve Historical Society, December, 1858.

Kennedy, James Harrison, *A History of the City of Cleveland.* Cleveland, Imperial, 1896.

Leading Manufacturers and Merchants of the City of Cleveland and Environs. 1836-1886. New York, International Publishing Co., 1886.

Orth, Samuel P., *History of Cleveland.* 3 volumes. Chicago, Clarke, 1910.

Post, Charles Asa, *Doan's Corners and the City Four Miles West.* Caxton, 1930.

Robison, W. Scott (ed.), *History of the City of Cleveland.* Cleveland, Robison and Crockett, 1887.

Rose, William Ganson, *Cleveland, the Making of a City.* Cleveland, World, 1950.

Whittlesey, Charles, *Early History of Cleveland.* Cleveland, Fairbanks and Benedict, 1867.

Whittlesey, Charles, *Subscription to the History of Cleveland. Mss. #145.* Western Reserve Historical Society, Cleveland, May 21, 1866.

Williams, Arthur B., *Geology of the Cleveland Region.* Cleveland, Museum of Natural History, 1940.

Wilson, Ella Grant, *Famous Old Euclid Avenue of Cleveland.* Cleveland, Evangelical press, 1932.

PART V   *Architecture in Ohio*

Frary, I. T., "Early Domestic Architecture in Ohio," *American Architect,* CXXIII (April 11, 1923), 307-312.

Frary, I. T., *Early Homes in Ohio.* Richmond, Garrett and Massie, 1936.

Knittle, Rhea Mansfield, *Early Ohio Taverns.* Ohio Frontier Series, 1937.

O'Donnell, Thomas Edward, "Influence of the Carpenter's Handbooks in the Early Architecture of Ohio," *Architecture,* LX (March, 1927), 169-71.

Roos, Frank John, Jr., "An Investigation of the Sources of Early Architectural Design in Ohio," *Abstracts of Doctoral Dissertations. No. 26,* Columbus, Ohio State University press, 1938.

Roos, Frank John, Jr., "Reflections of New England's Architecture in Ohio," *Old Time New England.* XXVIII (October, 1937), 40-48.

PART VI   *Architecture of the City of Cleveland*

Adams, Mary E., *First Baptist Church of Cleveland, Ohio. Historical sketch.* Cleveland, 1903.

Akers, William Joseph, *Cleveland Schools in the Nineteenth Century.* Cleveland, Bayre, 1901.

Annals of the First Presbyterian Church of Cleveland. 1820-1895. Cleveland, Winn and Judson, 1895.

Around the Public Square, 1849-1929. Society for Savings, City of Cleveland, 1929.

Baker, Samual J., "The Original Surveys of Cleveland," *Journal of the Association of Engineering Societies,* III, no. 10 (August, 1884), 217-232.

Baptist Churches, Cleveland, Ohio. (uncatalogued material). Western Reserve Historical Society.

Bourne, Henry E., *The Church of the Covenant. The First Hundred Years.* Cleveland, 1945.

Centennial Anniversary, 1846-1946, the Euclid Avenue Temple, Cleveland, Ohio. Cleveland, 1946.

Central High School Centennial. 1846-1946. May 10, 1946. Cleveland, 1946.

Church, Ransom M., "Notes on the History of St. John's Church, Cleveland," *Magazine of St. John's Parish.* Cleveland, 1909-10.

Cleveland Public Schools. Thirty-third Annual Report of the Board of Education for the School Year Ending Aug. 31, 1869. Cleveland, Fairbanks and Benedict, 1870.

Cully, John L., "The Cleveland Surveyor," *Journal of the Association of Engineering Societies,* III no. 10. (August, 1884), 269-275.

Denham, Joseph, *Changes in the Location of Churches in Cleveland, Ohio.* (typed manuscript in the Western Reserve University library), 1926.

Early History of the Second Presbyterian Church of Cleveland, Ohio. Mss. #740. Western Reserve Historical Society, n.d.

Euclid Avenue Baptist Church, Cleveland, Ohio. (uncatalogued material), Western Reserve Historical Society.

Fiftieth Anniversary Services of the Temple, Cleveland, Ohio. Tifereth Israel Congregation. 1900.

Frary, I. T., "The Passing of a Famous Avenue," *Architectural Record*, XLIII, no. 4 (April, 1918), 301-2.

Frary, I. T., (ed.), *Village Green to City Center.* Cleveland, 1943.

Fraser, John G., *A Century of Congregationalism in Cleveland.* Reprint from volume VIII of Papers of Ohio Church History Society, n.d.

Freese, Andrew, *Early History of the Cleveland Public Schools.* Cleveland, Robinson and Savage, 1876.

Griswold, Seneca O., "The Corporate Birth and Growth of Cleveland," *Western Reserve and Northern Ohio Historical Society. Tract no. 62.* (July 22, 1884).

Historic Sites of Cleveland. Hotels and Taverns. The Ohio Historical Records Survey Project, Columbus, 1942.

Historical Sketches. Seventy-five Years of the Euclid Avenue Baptist Church. Cleveland, Ohio. 1851-1926. Cleveland, Davis and Cannon, 1927.

History of the First Baptist Church of Cleveland, Ohio. 1833-1883. Cleveland, Savage, 1883.

History of the First Baptist Church, Cleveland, Ohio. 1833-1922. Cleveland, Schulte, 1922.

Hodge, Orlando J., "Cleveland's Early Hotels," *Orlando J. Hodge papers.* Mss #2823, no. 24, Western Reserve Historical Society.

Houck, George F., *A History of Catholicity in Northern Ohio and in the Diocese of Cleveland.* Cleveland, Savage, 1903.

Houck, George F., *The Church in Northern Ohio and in the Diocese of Cleveland, from 1817 to September, 1887.* New York, Benziger, 1887.

Grace Episcopal Church, Cleveland, Ohio (uncatalogued material). Western Reserve Historical Society.

Ludlow, A. C., and Mrs. A. C., *History of Cleveland Presbyterianism.* Cleveland, Bayne, 1896.

Ludlow, A. C., *The Old Stone Church. 1820-1920.* Cleveland, privately printed, 1920.

Manual and Catalogue of the Second Presbyterian Church in Cleveland, Ohio, from June 1844 to April 1864. Cleveland, Cowles, 1864.

Manual and Directory. First Presbyterian Church, Cleveland, Ohio. Cleveland, 1842.

Manual for the Communicants of the Second Presbyterian Church in Cleveland. Cleveland, Cowles, 1857.

Manual for the Members of the First Presbyterian Church in Cleveland. Cleveland, Smead, 1842.

Manual of the Plymouth Church, Cleveland, Ohio. Cleveland, Smead and Cowles, 1852.

Notice to perform 2 days labor on the streets. July 24, 1844. Mss. #2541. Western Reserve Historical Society.

Past and Present of Grace Church, Cleveland, Ohio. Cleveland, Williams, 1898.

Payne, William, *Cleveland Illustrated.* Cleveland, Fairbanks and Benedict, 1876.

Pease, Seth, "*Field Notes Made on the Connecticut Western Reserve, 1796.*" Western Reserve Historical Society.

"Pictures of the Fountain and Square, Light House, Court House, Medical College at Cleveland," *Ballou's Pictorial Drawing-room Companion*, XIII, (1857), 120-21.

Plymouth Church, Cleveland, Ohio, (uncatalogued material). Western Reserve Historical Society.

Pomeroy, Charles S., *An Historical Sketch Reviewing the Origin and Growth of the Second Presbyterian Church, Cleveland, Ohio.* Cleveland, Leader, 1876.

St. Paul's Episcopal Church, Cleveland. Records and Business Papers. Mss. #523. Western Reserve Historical Society.

Sargent, John H., *The Development of Cleveland's Harbor.* Cleveland, 1892.

Souvenir Directory, May 16-24, 1904. National Baptist Anniversaries, 1904. Cleveland, Ward and Shaw, 1904.

Souvenir of the First Presbyterian Church, Cleveland. Cleveland, Mount, n.d. (1886).

Trinity Cathedral, Cleveland. Historical and Architectural Guide. Cleveland, 1912.

Young, Ammi B., *Plans of Public Buildings in Course of Construction under the Direction of the Secretary of the Treasury, Including Specifications Thereof. Capt. A. H. Bowman, U. S. Corps of Engineers, and Engineer in Charge.* Treasury Dept. Washington 1855-6. No. 30. *Cleveland, Ohio, Custom House. Designed by A. B. Young, architect. 1856.*

PART VII   *Directories and Maps of the City of Cleveland*

Atlas of Cuyahoga County, Ohio, from Actual Surveys by and under the Direction of D. J. Lake, C. E. Philadelphia, Titus, Simmons and Titus, 1874.

Berry, Marriott and Bartlett, *Complete Business Directory of the City of Cleveland for 1857-58.* Cleveland, 1857.

Boyd, William Henry, *Boyd's Cleveland City Directory.* New York, Boyd, 1857.

Boyd, Andrew, *Boyd's Cleveland Directory and Cuyahoga County Business Directory. 1863-4.* Cleveland, Fairbanks and Benedict, 1863.

Cleveland Leader. Annual City Directory for 1868-69. Cleveland, Leader, 1868.

Ingham and Bragg, *Guide to the City of Cleveland.* Cleveland, 1860.

Insurance Maps of Cleveland, Ohio. New York, Sanborn, 1874-78.

Knight and Parsons, *Business Directory of the City of Cleveland.* Cleveland, Knight and Parsons, 1853.

MacCabe, Julius P. Bolivar, *A Directory of the Cities of Cleveland and Ohio, for the Years 1837-38.* Cleveland, Sandford and Lott, 1837.

Peet, Elijah, *Peet's General Business Directory of the Cities of Cleveland and Ohio for the Years 1845-6.* Cleveland, Sandford and Hayward, 1845.

Peet, Elijah, *Business Directory of the City of Cleveland for the Years 1846-7.* Cleveland, Smead and Cowles, 1846.

Peirce, M. P., *The Cleveland Almanac and Business Man's Directory for the Year 1857.* Cleveland, Peirce, 1857.

Smead and Cowles' General Business Directory of the City of Cleveland, for 1848-49. Compiled by Wm. Stephenson. Cleveland, Smead and Cowles, 1848.

Smead and Cowles' General Business Directory for the City of Cleveland. Compiled by I. N. Mason. Cleveland, Smead and Cowles, 1850.

Spear, Dennison & Co., *Cleveland City Directory for 1856.* Cleveland, Spear, Dennison, 1856.

Stringer and McArdle, *Cleveland City Guide for 1870.* Cleveland, Robison, 1870.

Williston, J. H., *Directory of the City of Cleveland for 1859-60.* Cleveland, Williston, n.d. [1859].

Williston, J. H., *Directory of the City of Cleveland for 1861-2.* Cleveland, Franklin, n.d. [1861].

PART VIII   *Bibliographies of American Architectural Books*

Hitchcock, Henry Russell, *American Architectural Books.* Minneapolis, University of Minnesota press, 1946.

Roos, Frank J., *Writings on Early American Architecture.* Columbus, Ohio State University press, 1943.

PART IX   *Architectural Handbooks*

Benjamin, Asher, *The Country Builder's Assistant.* Boston, Bangs, 1816.

Benjamin, Asher, *The American Builder's Companion.* Boston, Williams, 1827.

Benjamin, Asher, *The Builder's Guide.* Boston, Perkins and Marvin, 1839.

Brown, William, *The Carpenter's Assistant.* Worcester, Livermore, 1848.

Croff, G. B., *Model Suburban Architecture.* New York, 1870.

Downing, Andrew J., *The Architecture of Country Houses.* New York, Appleton, 1853.

Downing, Andrew J., *Cottage Residences.* New York, Wiley and Putnam, 1842.

Fairbairn, William, *On the Application of Cast Iron and Wrought Iron to Building Purposes.* New York, Wiley, 1854.

Hammond, J. H., *The Farmer's and Mechanic's Practical Architect.* Boston and Cleveland, Jewett, 1858.

Hopkins, John Henry, *Essay on Gothic Architecture, with Various Plans and Drawings for Churches.* Burlington, Vt., Smith and Harrington, 1836.

Shaw, Edward, *Civil Architecture.* Boston, Shaw and Stratton, 1832.

Shaw, Edward, *Rural Architecture.* Boston, Dow, 1843.

Sloan, Samuel, *City and Suburban Architecture.* Philadelphia, Lippincott, 1859.

Sloan, Samuel, *The Model Architect.* Philadelphia, Butler, 1860.

Walters, T. U., and Smith, J. J., *Cottage and Villa Architecture. Two Hundred Designs. No. 3.* Philadelphia, Carey and Hart, 1846.

PART X Descriptions of Cleveland in the *Annals of the Early Settler's Association of Cuyahoga County*

Cleveland, James D., "The City of Cleveland Sixty Years Ago," III, no. 5, 693-731.
Dibble, Lewis, "Personal Statement," II, no. 7, 48-58.
Hickox, Milo H., "Sixty Years Ago," III, no. 1, 75-6.
Merwin, George B., "Recollections," I, no. 5 14-23.
Merwin, George B., "Written Statement to the Early Settler's Association, May 20, 1880," I, no. 1, 64-70.
Morgan, I. A., "A Sketch of Pioneer Life," II, no. 11, 406-11.
Morgan, I. A., "What I Recollect," II, no. 2, appendix 59-65.
Rice, Harvey, "Autobiographical Address," III, no. 1, 35-42.
Spaulding, Rufus P., "Address," I, no. 1, 42.
Sprague, Ara, "Cleveland When a Village," I, no. 2, appendix, 74-77.
Watkins, George, "Early Days," II, no. 7, 14-21.
Williamson, S., "Rominiscences," I, no. 1, 54-58.

PART XI *Files of Newspapers*

The Cleveland Register. 1818-1820.
The Leader. 1819-1822, 1854-1875.
The Herald. 1823-1834, 1836-1837, 1839-1847.
The Whig. 1834-1836.
The Herald and Gazette. 1837-1838.
The Forest City Democrat. 1853-1854.
The Cleveland True Democrat. 1848-1853.

INDEX